Diabetic Dessert Cookbook

Step into a Realm of Exquisite Tastes and Textures with Desserts that Cater to your Dietary Needs, Making Every Meal a Celebration

Haley Andre

© Copyright 2024 by Haley Andre - All rights reserved. The following Book is reproduced below with the goal of providing information that is as accurate and reliable as possible. Regardless, purchasing this Book can be seen as consent to the fact that both the publisher and the author of this book are in no way experts on the topics discussed within and that any recommendations or suggestions that are made herein are for entertainment purposes only. Professionals should be consulted as needed prior to undertaking any of the action endorsed herein. This declaration is deemed fair and valid by both the American Bar Association and the Committee of Publishers Association and is legally binding throughout the United States. Furthermore, the transmission, duplication, or reproduction of any of the following work including specific information will be considered an illegal act irrespective of if it is done electronically or in print. This extends to creating a secondary or tertiary copy of the work or a recorded copy and is only allowed with the express written consent from the Publisher. All additional right reserved. The information in the following pages is broadly considered a truthful and accurate account of facts and as such, any inattention, use, or misuse of the information in question by the reader will render any resulting actions solely under their purview. There are no scenarios in which the publisher or the original author of this work can be in any fashion deemed liable for any hardship or damages that may befall them after undertaking information described herein. Additionally, the information in the following pages is intended only for informational purposes and should thus be thought of as universal. As befitting its nature, it is presented without assurance regarding its prolonged validity or interim quality. Trademarks that are mentioned are done without written consent and can in no way be considered an endorsement from the trademark holder.

Table of Contents

CHAPTER 1: UNDERSTANDING THE DIABETIC DIET 12
1.1 The Impact of Sugar on Blood Glucose Levels 12
1.2 Carbohydrates: Understanding the Basics 14
1.3 Balancing Your Diet: Tips for Incorporating Sweets 15
1.4 Sugar Substitute 17

CHAPTER 2: CAKES FOR EVERY OCCASION 21
2.1 Classic Vanilla Sponge Cake (Low-Carb Version) 21
Recipe 1: Almond Flour Vanilla Sponge Cake 21
Recipe 2: Keto Vanilla Cloud Cake 21
Recipe 3: Coconut Vanilla Sponge Delight 22
Recipe 4: Nutty Vanilla Sponge Cake 22
Recipe 5: Lemon-Infused Vanilla Sponge Cake 22

2.2 Decadent Chocolate Layer Cake (Sugar-Free) 23
Recipe 1: Keto Dark Chocolate Euphoria Cake 23
Recipe 2: Chocolate Velvet Symphony 23
Recipe 3: Sinless Chocolate Indulgence Cake 24
Recipe 4: Triple Chocolate Delight Cake 24
Recipe 5: Dark Chocolate Almond Bliss Cake 25

2.3 Zesty Lemon Drizzle Cake (Using Natural Sweeteners) 26
Recipe 1: Lemon Almond Bliss Cake 26
Recipe 2: Citrus Poppy Seed Cake 26
Recipe 3: Keto Lemon Coconut Cake 27
Recipe 4: Lemon Lavender Dream Cake 27
Recipe 5: Lemon Ginger Zing Cake 27

CHAPTER 3: DELIGHTFUL DIABETIC-FRIENDLY PIES 30
3.1 No-Sugar-Added Apple Pie 30
Recipe 1: Rustic Almond Apple Pie 30
Recipe 2: Granny's Keto Apple Pie 31
Recipe 3: Cinnamon Swirl Apple Tart 31
Recipe 4: Apple Pie in a Bowl 31

Recipe 5: Mini Apple Crisp Pies 32

3.2 RICH AND CREAMY PUMPKIN PIE (LOW-GI) 33

Recipe 1: Keto Pumpkin Custard Pie 33

Recipe 2: No-Bake Pumpkin Spice Mousse Pie 33

Recipe 3: Classic Pumpkin Pie with Almond Crust 33

Recipe 4: Pumpkin Cheesecake Pie 34

Recipe 5: Spiced Pumpkin Pie with Coconut Crust 34

3.3 SUMMER BERRY TART (GLUTEN-FREE)ù 35

Recipe 1: Almond Crust Berry Tart 35

Recipe 2: Coconut Flour Berry Tart 35

Recipe 3: No-Bake Berry Cashew Tart 35

Recipe 4: Hazelnut Chocolate Berry Tart 36

Recipe 5: Lemon Berry Flaxseed Tart 36

CHAPTER 4: COOKIES AND BISCOTTI 38

4.1 ALMOND FLOUR CHOCOLATE CHIP COOKIES 38

Recipe 1: Classic Almond Joy Cookies 38

Recipe 2: Cocoa Chip Almond Bites 38

Recipe 3: Almond Butter Choc-Chip Delights 39

Recipe 4: Vanilla Chocolate Chunk Cookies 39

Recipe 5: Nutty Chocolate Chip Almond Cookies 39

4.2 CRUNCHY PISTACHIO BISCOTTI (SUGAR-FREE) 40

Recipe 1: Classic Pistachio Almond Biscotti 40

Recipe 2: Lemon Zest Pistachio Biscotti 40

Recipe 3: Chocolate Dipped Pistachio Biscotti 41

Recipe 4: Orange Pistachio Biscotti 41

Recipe 5: Espresso Pistachio Biscotti 41

4.3 OATMEAL RAISIN COOKIES (SWEETENED WITH DATES) 42

Recipe 1: Date-Sweetened Oatmeal Delights 42

Recipe 2: Nutty Date Oat Cookies 42

Recipe 3: Date-Sweetened Cinnamon Raisin Cookies 43

Recipe 4: Simple Date Oatmeal Cookies 43

Recipe 5: Spiced Date and Oat Cookies 43

CHAPTER 5: BROWNIES AND BARS 46

5.1 FUDGY AVOCADO BROWNIES (LOW-CARB) 46
- *Recipe 1: Classic Avocado Cocoa Brownies* 46
- *Recipe 2: Avocado Espresso Brownies* 46
- *Recipe 3: Nutty Avocado Brownies* 47
- *Recipe 4: Avocado Mint Chocolate Brownies* 47
- *Recipe 5: Spicy Avocado Chocolate Brownies* 48

5.2 RASPBERRY OAT BARS (NO ADDED SUGAR) 49
- *Recipe 1: Raspberry Chia Oat Bars* 49
- *Recipe 2: Nutty Raspberry Oat Squares* 49
- *Recipe 3: Raspberry Oatmeal Breakfast Bars* 49
- *Recipe 4: Lemon Raspberry Oat Crumble Bars* 50

5.3 PEANUT BUTTER SWIRL CHOCOLATE BARS (KETO-FRIENDLY) 51
- *Recipe 1: Decadent Keto Peanut Butter Swirl Bars* 51
- *Recipe 2: Keto Peanut Butter Chocolate Dream Bars* 51
- *Recipe 3: Swirled Peanut Butter Keto Bars* 52
- *Recipe 4: Nutty Chocolate Peanut Butter Keto Squares* 52

CHAPTER 6: MUFFINS AND CUPCAKES 54

6.1 BLUEBERRY MUFFINS (SUGAR-FREE) 54
- *Recipe 1: Classic Keto Blueberry Muffins* 54
- *Recipe 2: Lemon Zest Blueberry Muffins* 54
- *Recipe 3: Nutty Blueberry Muffins* 55
- *Recipe 4: Cinnamon Swirl Blueberry Muffins* 56

6.2 CARROT CAKE CUPCAKES (WITH CREAM CHEESE FROSTING) 56
- *Recipe 1: Keto Carrot-Infused Cupcakes* 56
- *Recipe 2: Spiced Carrot Almond Cupcakes* 57
- *Recipe 3: Nutty Carrot Cake Minis* 58
- *Recipe 4: Classic Keto Carrot Cupcakes* 58

6.3 ZUCCHINI CHOCOLATE CHIP MUFFINS (LOW-CARB) 59
- *Recipe 1: Keto Zucchini Cocoa Nib Muffins* 59
- *Recipe 2: Zucchini Almond Chocolate Chip Muffins* 59
- *Recipe 3: Coconut Zucchini Chocolate Muffins* 59

Recipe 4: Zucchini Walnut Chocolate Muffins 60

CHAPTER 7: FROZEN DESSERTS 62

7.1 STRAWBERRY FROZEN YOGURT (NO-SUGAR-ADDED) 62

Recipe 1: Classic Creamy Strawberry Frozen Yogurt 62

Recipe 2: Strawberry Basil Frozen Yogurt 62

Recipe 3: Strawberry Coconut Frozen Yogurt 62

Recipe 4: Minty Strawberry Frozen Yogurt 63

7.2 CHOCOLATE PEANUT BUTTER ICE CREAM (LOW-CARB) 63

Recipe 1: Keto Double Chocolate Peanut Butter Swirl 63

Recipe 2: Peanut Butter Fudge Ripple Ice Cream 64

Recipe 3: No-Churn Chocolate Peanut Butter Delight 64

Recipe 4: Creamy Peanut Butter Cocoa Ice Cream 64

7.3 MANGO SORBET (NATURALLY SWEETENED) 65

Recipe 1: Tropical Mango Lime Sorbet 65

Recipe 2: Mango Basil Sorbet 66

Recipe 3: Spiced Mango Sorbet 66

Recipe 4: Mango Coconut Sorbet 67

BONUS: Gourmet Breakfast Bliss Guide 68

CHAPTER 8: PUDDINGS AND PARFAITS 69

8.1 CHIA SEED PUDDING (VARIETY OF FLAVORS) 69

Recipe 1: Vanilla Bean Chia Pudding 69

Recipe 2: Berry Bliss Chia Pudding 69

Recipe 3: Cinnamon Spice Chia Pudding 70

Recipe 4: Tropical Mango Coconut Chia Pudding 70

8.2 LAYERED FRUIT AND YOGURT PARFAIT (SUGAR-FREE) 70

Recipe 1: Berry Almond Yogurt Parfait 70

Recipe 2: Tropical Coconut Mango Parfait 71

Recipe 3: Cinnamon Apple Crunch Parfait 71

Recipe 4: Peach Pecan Yogurt Parfait 72

8.3 RICH CHOCOLATE PUDDING (AVOCADO-BASED) 72

Recipe 1: Classic Avocado Chocolate Pudding 72

Recipe 2: Mocha Avocado Chocolate Pudding 72

Recipe 3: Raspberry Avocado Chocolate Pudding 73

Recipe 4: Nutty Avocado Chocolate Pudding 73

CHAPTER 9: FESTIVE DESSERTS 75

9.1 DIABETIC-FRIENDLY CHRISTMAS YULE LOG 75

Recipe 1: Classic Keto Yule Log 75

Recipe 2: No-Bake Chocolate Peppermint Yule Log 75

Recipe 3: Espresso Almond Yule Log 76

Recipe 4: Nutty Pumpkin Spice Yule Log 76

9.2 NO-BAKE CHEESECAKE (FOR EASTER CELEBRATIONS) 77

Recipe 1: Lemon Berry Keto Cheesecake 77

Recipe 2: Vanilla Bean Coconut Cheesecake 78

Recipe 3: Chocolate Hazelnut Cheesecake 78

Recipe 4: Strawberry Pistachio Cheesecake 78

9.3 PUMPKIN SPICE CUSTARDS (THANKSGIVING TREAT) 79

Recipe 1: Classic Keto Pumpkin Custard 79

Recipe 2: Spiced Coconut Milk Pumpkin Custard 79

Recipe 3: Nutmeg-Infused Pumpkin Custard 80

Recipe 4: Pumpkin Almond Custard 80

CHAPTER 10: INTERNATIONAL DESSERTS 82

10.1 ITALIAN TIRAMISU (ADJUSTED FOR DIABETICS) 82

Recipe 1: Classic Diabetic-Friendly Tiramisu 82

Recipe 2: No-Coffee Berry Tiramisu 82

Recipe 3: Espresso Walnut Tiramisu 83

Recipe 4: Chocolate Orange Tiramisu 83

10.2 FRENCH CLAFOUTIS WITH DARK CHERRIES (SUGAR SUBSTITUTE) 84

Recipe 1: Keto Cherry Clafoutis 84

Recipe 2: Coconut Flour Cherry Clafoutis 85

Recipe 3: Lemon Zest Cherry Clafoutis 85

Recipe 4: Dark Chocolate Cherry Clafoutis 85

10.3 INDIAN CARROT HALWA (MADE WITH ARTIFICIAL SWEETENER) 86

Recipe 1: Classic Keto Carrot Halwa 86

Recipe 2: Vegan Coconut Carrot Halwa 86

Recipe 3: Saffron-Infused Carrot Halwa 87

Recipe 4: Nutty Carrot Halwa 87

CHAPTER 11: SMOOTHIES AND DRINKS **89**

11.1 GREEN DETOX SMOOTHIE (WITH SPINACH AND AVOCADO) 89

Recipe 1: Classic Spinach Avocado Detox Smoothie 89

Recipe 2: Ginger-Lime Green Smoothie 89

Recipe 3: Creamy Kale and Avocado Smoothie 89

Recipe 4: Avocado Spinach Protein Smoothie 90

11.2 ALMOND MILK HOT CHOCOLATE (SUGAR-FREE) 90

Recipe 1: Classic Creamy Almond Milk Hot Chocolate 90

Recipe 2: Spiced Almond Milk Hot Chocolate 91

Recipe 3: Minty Almond Milk Hot Cocoa 91

Recipe 4: Lavender Almond Milk Hot Chocolate 91

11.3 BERRY BLAST SMOOTHIE (NO ADDED SUGAR) 92

Recipe 1: Ultimate Berry Almond Smoothie 92

Recipe 2: Berry Avocado Glow Smoothie 92

Recipe 3: Refreshing Berry Mint Smoothie 93

Recipe 4: Berry Ginger Zing Smoothie 93

CHAPTER 12: CONCLUSION **95**

12.1 EMBRACING A SWEET LIFE WITHOUT SUGAR 95

12.2 THE IMPORTANCE OF PORTION CONTROL 96

12.3 INCORPORATING NATURAL SWEETNESS 97

12.4 LOOKING AHEAD 99

Chapter 1: Understanding the Diabetic Diet

1.1 The Impact of Sugar on Blood Glucose Levels

When we embark on the journey of understanding the diabetic diet, the role of sugar in influencing blood glucose levels emerges as a fundamental starting point. This exploration is not just about identifying the culprits in our diet; it's about redefining our relationship with food, particularly with sweets, which have long been vilified in the narrative of diabetes management.

Sugar, in its most basic form, is a carbohydrate. When we consume foods containing this sweet substance, our body breaks it down into glucose, which enters our bloodstream. This process is natural and necessary, as glucose serves as a primary energy source for our cells. However, the plot thickens when we introduce the concept of insulin, a hormone produced by the pancreas. Insulin acts as a key, unlocking our cells so that glucose can enter and be used for energy. In individuals with diabetes, this process is disrupted. Elevated blood glucose levels result from either insufficient insulin production or inefficient insulin utilization by the body.

The impact of sugar on blood glucose levels is not a tale of mere cause and effect; it's a complex interplay of quantity, quality, and timing. The type of sugar consumed plays a crucial role. Simple sugars, found in sweets, sodas, and processed foods, are absorbed quickly into the bloodstream, causing rapid spikes in blood glucose levels. These spikes can be particularly problematic for individuals managing diabetes, as they require the body to rapidly manage large amounts of glucose.

Conversely, complex carbohydrates, found in whole grains, vegetables, and legumes, are broken down more slowly, resulting in a more gradual release of glucose into the bloodstream. This slow and steady approach is preferable for blood glucose management, as it helps avoid the sharp peaks and valleys that can complicate diabetes control.

The quantity of sugar consumed is another critical factor. It's not just about avoiding the sugar bowl; it's about understanding the hidden sugars that lurk in many processed foods. Labels reading "low-fat" or "healthy" can be misleading, masking the high sugar content that often compensates for reduced fat. Awareness and education on reading food labels become indispensable tools in managing blood glucose levels.

Timing also plays a pivotal role. Consuming sugary foods or beverages on an empty stomach can lead to quicker absorption and more pronounced blood glucose spikes. In contrast, incorporating a sweet treat into a balanced meal, which includes fiber, fat, and protein, can mitigate this effect, slowing the absorption of sugar and providing a more gentle impact on blood glucose levels.

The narrative surrounding sugar and diabetes is often fraught with fear and restriction. But knowing how sugar affects blood glucose levels shouldn't be used to demonize sugar—rather, it should arm people with the information they need to make wise decisions.

It's about finding balance and moderation in a diet that supports blood glucose management without sacrificing the joy of eating.

This journey of understanding does not advocate for a sugar-free existence but rather for a mindful approach to consumption. It's about realizing that, if eaten in moderation, occasional sugary treats can fit within a balanced, well-rounded diabetic diet.

In navigating the diabetic diet, the relationship with sugar is not one of avoidance but of understanding. It's about learning to listen to our bodies, recognizing the signals of blood glucose fluctuations, and adjusting our intake accordingly. It's a dance of balance, where the rhythm is dictated by the complex interplay of food, metabolism, and insulin.

As we peel back the layers of this relationship, we uncover not just the challenges but also the opportunities for creativity and innovation in the kitchen. The quest for managing blood glucose levels becomes an invitation to explore new flavors, textures, and ingredients that not only nourish the body but also delight the palate.

In this context, sugar ceases to be the enemy. Instead, it becomes a character in a larger story of health and wellness, where every food choice is an opportunity to support our bodies in managing diabetes. It's a narrative that embraces the full spectrum of eating experiences, recognizing that the path to health is not paved with deprivation but with informed, mindful choices.

Recognizing how sugar affects blood sugar is the first step towards redefining the diabetic diet as a platform for creative cooking and individual well-being rather than as a set of limitations.

It's a journey that invites us to explore, experiment, and enjoy, all while keeping our health and well-being at the forefront.

1.2 Carbohydrates: Understanding the Basics

Carbohydrates, often simply called carbs, form one of the fundamental food groups necessary for a balanced diet. Yet, in the context of managing diabetes, carbohydrates take on a more nuanced role, necessitating a deeper understanding than the typical "good vs. bad" narrative often presented in popular media. This exploration into the basics of carbohydrates aims to demystify this essential macronutrient, providing a foundation for making informed dietary choices that support diabetes management.

The main source of energy for the body is glucose, which comes in both basic and complicated forms. Simple carbohydrates, also known as simple sugars, are found in meals like fruit and milk as well as less healthy items like candy and manufactured sweets. Because they are easily absorbed, simple sugars can lead to sharp spikes in blood glucose levels. Conversely, whole grains, legumes, and vegetables contain complex carbs. Their slower breakdown results in a consistent energy source and a more gradual impact on blood glucose levels.

Understanding carbohydrates requires more than just distinguishing between simple and complex. It's about recognizing the role of fiber, the importance of the glycemic index, and the overall impact of carbohydrate consumption on blood glucose management.

Fiber, a type of carbohydrate that the body can't digest, plays a critical role in managing diabetes. Vegetables, fruits, whole grains, and legumes are examples of foods high in fiber that can help slow down the absorption of sugar and help maintain more stable blood glucose levels.

Incorporating these fiber-rich foods into a diabetic diet is not just about managing blood sugar; it's also about supporting overall digestive health and providing a sense of fullness, which can help with weight management.

The glycemic index (GI) is another critical concept in understanding carbohydrates. The GI gauges the pace at which a meal high in carbohydrates elevates blood glucose levels. Foods with a low GI absorb more slowly, causing blood glucose levels to rise gradually, whereas foods with a high GI absorb fast, causing sudden spikes in blood glucose levels. In a diabetic diet, a focus on low-GI foods can aid in better blood glucose control.

But understanding carbohydrates in the context of diabetes isn't just about the type of carbs consumed; it's also about the amount. Carbohydrate counting, or carb counting, is a method used by many individuals with diabetes to manage their blood glucose levels. This approach involves keeping track of the number of carbohydrates consumed at each meal to maintain blood glucose levels within a target range.

This nuanced understanding of carbohydrates also necessitates a reevaluation of the diet as a whole. It's not merely about eliminating certain foods but about creating a balanced, varied diet that supports blood glucose management while also providing nutritional completeness. In order to further limit the absorption of glucose into the bloodstream and guarantee a more constant blood glucose level, this entails combining carbohydrates with healthful fats and proteins.

Moreover, understanding carbohydrates is also about dispelling myths and misconceptions. Carbohydrates are often seen as the enemy in the context of diabetes, but when chosen carefully and consumed in moderation, they are an essential part of a healthy diet. It's about quality and balance, not deprivation.

The role of carbohydrates in a diabetic diet is a dynamic interplay between the type of carbs, the amount consumed, and their interaction with other nutrients. This complexity doesn't have to be overwhelming. By embracing a holistic approach to carbohydrate consumption, individuals with diabetes can enjoy a diverse and satisfying diet while effectively managing their blood glucose levels.

In sum, carbohydrates play a pivotal role in the diabetic diet, serving as both a primary energy source and a critical factor in blood glucose management. Understanding the basics of carbohydrates – the difference between simple and complex carbs, the importance of fiber, the relevance of the glycemic index, and the practice of carbohydrate counting – provides a solid foundation for dietary decision-making. This knowledge empowers individuals with diabetes to navigate their dietary choices with confidence, ensuring that carbohydrates are consumed in a way that supports their overall health and well-being.

1.3 Balancing Your Diet: Tips for Incorporating Sweets

Navigating a diabetic diet often feels like walking a tightrope, where the balance between managing blood glucose levels and indulging in the sweetness of life becomes a daily performance. The common misconception that a diagnosis of diabetes means a life devoid of dessert is not only outdated but far from the truth. The secret lies in understanding how to incorporate sweets into your diet in a way that maintains this delicate balance. Here, we explore strategies that allow for the enjoyment of sweets while ensuring that health remains a top priority.

First and foremost, the concept of moderation cannot be overstressed. Enjoying sweets in small quantities is a cornerstone of a balanced diabetic diet. This approach allows for the occasional indulgence without significantly impacting blood glucose levels. It's about savoring the flavor, not the quantity, transforming a potentially guilt-ridden experience into a mindful and enjoyable moment.

Pairing sweets with healthy nutrients is another effective strategy for minimizing their impact on blood glucose. When sweets are consumed alongside meals or snacks that are high in fiber, protein, or healthy fats, the absorption of sugar into the bloodstream is slowed. This pairing not only helps to prevent spikes in blood glucose but also contributes to a more satisfying eating experience, as it combines the pleasure of sweetness with the satiety provided by more nutrient-dense foods.

Understanding the glycemic index (GI) of foods can also play a critical role in incorporating sweets into a diabetic diet. Opting for desserts that are lower on the glycemic index can make a significant difference in how they affect your blood glucose levels. Ingredients such as fruits that are lower in natural sugars and high in fiber, like berries, can be excellent choices for creating low-GI sweet treats.

Another valuable tip is to become creative in the kitchen. Preparing your own desserts allows for complete control over the ingredients and portions. This DIY approach enables the substitution of traditional, high-sugar ingredients with healthier alternatives, such as using natural sweeteners like stevia or incorporating whole grains and nuts for added fiber and nutrients. The internet abounds with diabetic-friendly dessert recipes that emphasize flavor without compromising health.

Timing also plays a pivotal role in how sweets impact blood glucose levels. Incorporating a small dessert as part of a meal, rather than as a standalone snack, can help mitigate its effect on your blood sugar. This strategy leverages the balancing act of nutrients from the meal to moderate the absorption of sugar, aligning with the body's natural metabolic processes.

Staying active is another key component of balancing a diet that includes sweets. Frequent exercise improves the body's ability to utilise insulin, which can aid with blood glucose management.

Engaging in a post-meal walk or any form of exercise can be particularly beneficial after indulging in a sweet treat, as it aids in stabilizing blood sugar by increasing glucose uptake by the muscles.

Monitoring blood glucose levels closely is indispensable when incorporating sweets into a diabetic diet. This vigilance allows for real-time feedback on how different types of sweets and the strategies employed to balance them affect your blood glucose. Keeping a food diary can be incredibly helpful in identifying patterns and making informed adjustments to your diet.

Finally, fostering a mindset that views food as a friend, not a foe, is crucial. Deprivation can lead to cravings, which can culminate in overindulgence. By allowing yourself the occasional sweet treat within the framework of a balanced diet, you create a sustainable approach to diabetes management that embraces enjoyment rather than restriction.

Incorporating sweets into a diabetic diet is an art that balances science with pleasure. It requires mindfulness, creativity, and a deep understanding of how different foods interact with your body. By employing these strategies, individuals with diabetes can enjoy the sweetness of life without compromising their health, proving that a diagnosis does not dictate deprivation but rather invites innovation in the pursuit of balance and wellness.

1.4 Sugar Substitute

In the landscape of a diabetic diet, sugar substitutes emerge as a beacon of hope and a source of contention. These alternatives to traditional sugar promise the sweetness we crave without the accompanying spike in blood glucose levels, offering a semblance of normalcy in a diet often marked by restrictions. Yet, navigating the world of sugar substitutes is not without its challenges, as each option brings its own benefits and considerations. This exploration into sugar substitutes is not just about finding alternatives to sugar; it's about understanding their impact on health, blood glucose management, and the culinary possibilities they unlock.

Sugar substitutes, broadly categorized into artificial sweeteners, sugar alcohols, and natural sweeteners, each have a unique chemical makeup and effect on the body. Artificial sweeteners, such as aspartame and sucralose, are synthetic options that provide intense sweetness without the calories or carbohydrates of sugar. Their potency allows them to be used in minuscule amounts, making them a popular choice for beverages and packaged foods designed for weight loss or diabetes management. However, their use is often shadowed by debates over safety and potential health risks, despite approval from health authorities.

Sugar alcohols, including xylitol and erythritol, offer a middle ground, with fewer calories than sugar and a lower impact on blood glucose levels. Their presence in chewing gums, sugar-free candies, and baked goods provides a sweet alternative that can minimize blood sugar spikes. Yet, their gastrointestinal side effects, such as bloating and diarrhea when consumed in large amounts, necessitate moderation.

Natural sweeteners, like stevia and monk fruit extract, are derived from plants and have gained popularity for their minimal impact on blood glucose levels and natural origin. Their appeal lies not only in their sweetness but also in their perceived health benefits over synthetic options.

However, the variability in flavor and aftertaste, coupled with their cost, can limit their use in some culinary applications.

Examining the glycemic index (GI) of sugar alternatives is necessary to comprehend their subtleties because it indicates how much a food high in carbohydrates elevates blood sugar levels. Unlike regular sugar with a high GI, most sugar substitutes have a low or negligible effect on blood glucose, making them attractive for diabetes management. However, the effectiveness of these substitutes in controlling blood glucose levels extends beyond their GI; it also depends on how they are used in the context of a balanced diet.

Incorporating sugar substitutes into a diabetic diet offers an opportunity to enjoy sweet flavors without compromising blood glucose control. However, it's essential to consider the overall nutritional profile of foods containing these substitutes. Products labeled as "sugar-free" or "no added sugar" are not inherently calorie-free or healthy and may contain other ingredients that impact blood glucose levels or overall health.

Moreover, the psychological aspect of using sugar substitutes cannot be overlooked. The ability to enjoy sweet flavors without the associated rise in blood glucose can positively affect one's quality of life and adherence to a diabetic diet. Yet, there's a risk of overindulgence in foods containing sugar substitutes under the guise of them being "safe," potentially leading to unwanted calorie consumption and weight gain.

The culinary application of sugar substitutes is another realm of exploration. While they can mimic the sweetness of sugar, their varying properties mean they may not behave the same way in recipes, particularly in baking, where sugar plays a crucial role in texture and volume. Experimentation and adjustment are often necessary to achieve the desired results, with some substitutes better suited for certain applications than others.

In navigating the use of sugar substitutes, education and personal experimentation become paramount. Understanding the types of substitutes available, their impact on blood glucose levels, and how to incorporate them into a diet without compromising nutritional quality or taste is crucial. Consulting with healthcare professionals, particularly for individuals with diabetes, ensures that the use of these substitutes aligns with overall health goals and blood glucose management strategies.

In conclusion, sugar substitutes offer a complex but promising tool in the management of diabetes, allowing for the enjoyment of sweet flavors without the direct impact on blood glucose levels associated with sugar. Their diverse range, from artificial sweeteners to natural options, provides choices to suit different preferences and needs. Yet, their successful incorporation into a diabetic diet requires a balanced approach that considers their nutritional impact, psychological effects, and culinary applications. As we continue to explore the possibilities and limitations of sugar substitutes, their role in a diabetic diet remains a testament to the ongoing evolution of our understanding of nutrition, health, and the pursuit of sweetness in a life with diabetes.

Chapter 2: Cakes for Every Occasion

2.1 Classic Vanilla Sponge Cake (Low-Carb Version)

Recipe 1: Almond Flour Vanilla Sponge Cake

P.T.: 35 mins

Ingr.: 2 Cups almond flour, quarter Cup coconut flour, 1 tsp baking powder, half tsp salt, 6 large eggs, separated, quarter Cup unsweetened almond milk, 2 tsp vanilla extract, 1/3 Cup erythritol, quarter tsp cream of tartar.

Serves: 8

M.C.: Baking

Procedure: Begin by preheating your oven to 325°F (163°C) and greasing a 9-inch cake pan. In a bowl, mix almond flour, coconut flour, baking powder, and salt. In a separate bowl, whisk egg yolks, almond milk, and vanilla extract until smooth. Gradually add erythritol to the yolk mixture. Combine dry and wet ingredients. In another bowl, beat egg whites and cream of tartar to stiff peaks. Gently fold into the batter. Pour into the pan and bake for 25-30 mins until a toothpick comes out clean.

N.V.: Approx. 3g net carbs per serving.

Recipe 2: Keto Vanilla Cloud Cake

P.T.: 40 mins

Ingr.: 3 Cups almond flour, 1 tbsp baking powder, half tsp salt, half Cup melted unsalted butter, 1 Cup granulated Swerve, 5 large eggs, 3/4 Cup heavy cream, 1 tbsp vanilla extract.

Serves: 10

M.C.: Baking

Procedure: Preheat the oven to 350°F (177°C). Combine almond flour, baking powder, and salt in a bowl. In another bowl, mix melted butter and Swerve. Add eggs one at a time, then stir in heavy cream and vanilla extract. Gradually mix in dry ingredients. Pour batter into a greased 9-inch round cake pan. Bake for 30-35 mins. Let cool before serving.

N.V.: Around 2.5g net carbs per serving.

Recipe 3: Coconut Vanilla Sponge Delight

P.T.: 50 mins

Ingr.: 1 half Cups coconut flour, 1 tsp baking soda, quarter tsp Himalayan pink salt, 8 large eggs, half Cup melted coconut oil, half Cup unsweetened coconut milk, 2/3 Cup erythritol, 2 tsp pure vanilla extract.

Serves: 12

M.C.: Baking

Procedure: Start by preheating your oven to 350°F (177°C). Sift together coconut flour, baking soda, and salt. Beat eggs, coconut oil, coconut milk, erythritol, and vanilla extract until smooth. Slowly incorporate dry ingredients into wet, mixing until well combined. Pour the batter into a lined and greased 9-inch cake pan. Bake for 35-40 mins. Cool before slicing.

N.V.: Approximately 4g net carbs per serving.

Recipe 4: Nutty Vanilla Sponge Cake

P.T.: 45 mins

Ingr.: 2 half Cups finely ground mixed nuts (almonds, walnuts, pecans), 1 tsp baking powder, quarter tsp salt, half Cup melted butter, 3/4 Cup erythritol, 4 large eggs, half Cup unsweetened almond milk, 1 tsp vanilla bean paste.

Serves: 8

M.C.: Baking

Procedure: Preheat your oven to 325°F (163°C). Mix ground nuts, baking powder, and salt. In another bowl, whisk melted butter and erythritol until creamy. Add eggs, one at a time, then almond milk and vanilla bean paste. Combine with dry ingredients. Pour into a prepared 9-inch cake pan. Bake for 30 mins. Test with a toothpick for doneness. Allow to cool before serving.

N.V.: About 3g net carbs per slice.

Recipe 5: Lemon-Infused Vanilla Sponge Cake

P.T.: 38 mins

Ingr.: 2 Cups almond flour, half Cup coconut flour, 1 tsp baking powder, quarter tsp sea salt, 6 eggs, half Cup unsweetened almond milk, half Cup erythritol, zest of 1 lemon, 2 tsp vanilla extract, quarter Cup olive oil.

Serves: 10

M.C.: Baking

Procedure: Preheat oven to 350°F (177°C). Whisk together almond flour, coconut flour, baking powder, and salt. In a separate bowl, beat eggs with almond milk, erythritol, lemon zest, vanilla extract, and olive oil until smooth. Gradually add dry ingredients to wet, mixing until just combined. Pour into a greased 9-inch round cake pan. Bake for 25-30 mins or until a toothpick inserted comes out clean. Cool before serving.

N.V.: Less than 5g net carbs per serving.

2.2 Decadent Chocolate Layer Cake (Sugar-Free)

Recipe 1: Keto Dark Chocolate Euphoria Cake

P.T.: 60 mins

Ingr.: 2 Cups almond flour, 3/4 Cup unsweetened cocoa powder, half Cup coconut flour, 1 tsp baking powder, 1 tsp baking soda, quarter tsp salt, 1 Cup unsweetened almond milk, 3/4 Cup erythritol, 4 large eggs, 2 tsp vanilla extract, 1 Cup melted coconut oil.

Serves: 12

M.C.: Baking

Procedure: Begin by preheating your oven to 350°F (177°C). Mix almond flour, cocoa powder, coconut flour, baking powder, baking soda, and salt. In another bowl, combine almond milk, erythritol, eggs, vanilla extract, and melted coconut oil. Merge the dry and wet ingredients. Pour into two greased 9-inch round cake pans. Bake for 25-30 mins. Allow to cool before layering.

N.V.: Approx. 5g net carbs per serving.

Recipe 2: Chocolate Velvet Symphony

P.T.: 45 mins

Ingr.: 3 Cups ground walnuts, 1 Cup unsweetened cocoa powder, half tsp salt, 1 tsp instant coffee powder, 1 Cup erythritol, 6 eggs, separated, half Cup unsalted butter, melted, 2 tsp vanilla extract.

Serves: 10

M.C.: Baking

Procedure: Preheat the oven to 325°F (163°C). Combine ground walnuts, cocoa powder, salt, and coffee powder. Beat egg yolks with erythritol, melted butter, and vanilla until creamy. In another bowl, whip egg whites to stiff peaks. Fold the walnut mixture into the yolk mixture, then gently fold in egg whites. Divide batter among two greased 9-inch pans. Bake for 20 mins. Cool before assembling.

N.V.: Only 4g net carbs per serving.

Recipe 3: Sinless Chocolate Indulgence Cake

P.T.: 70 mins

Ingr.: 2 half Cups almond flour, 1 Cup unsweetened cocoa powder, 1 tsp baking powder, half tsp Himalayan pink salt, 3/4 Cup melted coconut oil, 1 Cup powdered erythritol, 5 large eggs, 1 tsp vanilla essence, 1 Cup boiling water.

Serves: 12

M.C.: Baking

Procedure: Start by preheating your oven to 350°F (177°C). Whisk together almond flour, cocoa powder, baking powder, and salt. In a separate bowl, mix coconut oil, erythritol, eggs, and vanilla essence until smooth. Gradually add dry ingredients to wet, then stir in boiling water until the batter is smooth. Pour into two greased 9-inch cake pans and bake for 30-35 mins. Let cool prior to layering.

N.V.: Approximately 3g net carbs per serving.

Recipe 4: Triple Chocolate Delight Cake

P.T.: 55 mins

Ingr.: 1 half Cups hazelnut flour, 1 Cup unsweetened cocoa powder, quarter Cup coconut flour, 1 tsp baking soda, half tsp salt, 1 Cup unsweetened almond milk, 2/3 Cup erythritol, 4 eggs, 2 tsp vanilla extract, half Cup avocado oil, half Cup sugar-free dark chocolate chips.

Serves: 10

M.C.: Baking

Procedure: Preheat oven to 350°F (177°C). Mix hazelnut flour, cocoa powder, coconut flour, baking soda, and salt. In another bowl, whisk almond milk, erythritol, eggs, vanilla extract, and avocado oil. Combine wet and dry ingredients, then fold in chocolate chips. Split batter into two 9-inch cake pans. Bake for 25-28 mins. Cool before assembling.

N.V.: Less than 6g net carbs per serving.

Recipe 5: Dark Chocolate Almond Bliss Cake

P.T.: 50 mins

Ingr.: 2 Cups almond flour, half Cup unsweetened dark cocoa powder, 1 tsp baking powder, half Cup melted dark chocolate (sugar-free), half Cup erythritol, half tsp sea salt, 4 large eggs, half Cup unsweetened almond milk, quarter Cup olive oil, 2 tsp almond extract.

Serves: 12

M.C.: Baking

Procedure: Heat oven to 350°F (177°C). Stir together almond flour, cocoa powder, and baking powder. Melt dark chocolate, then mix with erythritol, sea salt, eggs, almond milk, olive oil, and almond extract until smooth. Gradually blend in dry ingredients. Divide the batter between two 9-inch cake pans, greased. Bake for 25-30 mins. Allow to cool before layering.

N.V.: Approximately 5g net carbs per slice.

2.3 Zesty Lemon Drizzle Cake (Using Natural Sweeteners)

Recipe 1: Lemon Almond Bliss Cake

P.T.: 45 mins

Ingr.: 2 Cups almond flour, quarter Cup coconut flour, 1 tsp baking powder, half tsp salt, 4 eggs, half Cup unsweetened almond milk, 1/3 Cup erythritol, zest of 2 lemons, juice of 1 lemon, quarter Cup melted coconut oil, 1 tsp vanilla extract.

Serves: 8

M.C.: Baking

Procedure: Preheat oven to 350°F (177°C). Whisk together almond flour, coconut flour, baking powder, and salt. In a separate bowl, beat eggs with almond milk, erythritol, lemon zest, lemon juice, melted coconut oil, and vanilla extract until smooth. Combine dry and wet ingredients. Pour into a greased 9-inch round cake pan. Bake for 30 mins. Cool before drizzling with additional lemon juice mixed with erythritol.

N.V.: Approx. 3g net carbs per serving.

Recipe 2: Citrus Poppy Seed Cake

P.T.: 50 mins

Ingr.: 1 half Cups almond flour, half Cup erythritol, quarter Cup coconut flour, 2 tsp baking powder, quarter tsp salt, 4 large eggs, half Cup unsweetened almond milk, zest of 3 lemons, quarter Cup lemon juice, half Cup melted butter, 2 tbsp poppy seeds, 1 tsp vanilla extract.

Serves: 10

M.C.: Baking

Procedure: Preheat the oven to 350°F (177°C). Mix almond flour, erythritol, coconut flour, baking powder, and salt. In another bowl, whisk together eggs, almond milk, lemon zest, lemon juice, melted butter, and vanilla. Stir in dry ingredients until well combined. Fold in poppy seeds. Pour batter into a lined loaf pan. Bake for 40 mins. Drizzle with a lemon juice and erythritol glaze after cooling.

N.V.: Around 4g net carbs per serving.

Recipe 3: Keto Lemon Coconut Cake

P.T.: 55 mins

Ingr.: 2 Cups almond flour, 1/3 Cup erythritol, half Cup shredded unsweetened coconut, 1 tsp baking powder, half tsp salt, 5 eggs, half Cup coconut oil, melted, zest of 2 lemons, half Cup lemon juice, 1 tsp vanilla extract.

Serves: 12

M.C.: Baking

Procedure: Start by preheating your oven to 350°F (177°C). Combine almond flour, erythritol, shredded coconut, baking powder, and salt in a bowl. In a separate bowl, mix eggs, melted coconut oil, lemon zest, lemon juice, and vanilla extract. Gradually mix wet ingredients into dry until smooth. Pour into a greased 9-inch cake pan. Bake for 35 mins. Let cool before serving with a lemon zest garnish.

N.V.: Less than 5g net carbs per slice.

Recipe 4: Lemon Lavender Dream Cake

P.T.: 60 mins

Ingr.: 2 quarter Cups almond flour, quarter Cup erythritol, 1 tsp baking powder, quarter tsp sea salt, 6 eggs, half Cup unsweetened almond milk, half Cup olive oil, zest of 3 lemons, quarter Cup lemon juice, 1 tsp vanilla extract, 1 tbsp dried lavender flowers.

Serves: 10

M.C.: Baking

Procedure: Preheat the oven to 325°F (163°C). Whisk almond flour, erythritol, baking powder, salt, and lavender. In another bowl, beat eggs, almond milk, olive oil, lemon zest, lemon juice, and vanilla until well combined. Fold wet ingredients into dry. Pour into two greased 8-inch round cake pans. Bake for 25 mins. Cool before layering and serving with a lemon and erythritol drizzle.

N.V.: Approximately 3g net carbs per serving.

Recipe 5: Lemon Ginger Zing Cake

P.T.: 48 mins

Ingr.: 2 Cups almond flour, half Cup erythritol, 1 tsp ground ginger, 1 tsp baking powder, half tsp salt, 4 eggs, quarter Cup unsweetened almond milk, half Cup melted butter, zest of 2 lemons, quarter Cup fresh lemon juice, 1 tsp vanilla extract, 2 tbsp grated fresh ginger.

Serves: 8

M.C.: Baking

Procedure: Preheat oven to 350°F (177°C). Mix almond flour, erythritol, ground ginger, baking powder, and salt. In a separate bowl, whisk eggs, almond milk, melted butter, lemon zest, lemon juice, vanilla, and grated ginger until smooth. Combine with dry ingredients. Pour into a greased 9-inch round cake pan. Bake for 28-32 mins. Cool before topping with a lemon zest and erythritol mixture.

N.V.: Around 4g net carbs per serving.

Chapter 3: Delightful Diabetic-Friendly Pies

3.1 No-Sugar-Added Apple Pie

Recipe 1: Rustic Almond Apple Pie

P.T.: 1 hour 20 mins

Ingr.: 3 Cups blanched almond flour, half Cup cold butter (cubed), 1 egg, 4 medium apples (thinly sliced), 1 tsp cinnamon, quarter tsp nutmeg, quarter Cup erythritol, zest of 1 lemon.

Serves: 8

M.C.: Baking

Procedure: Mix almond flour and cold butter in a food processor until crumbly. Add the egg to form a dough. Press two-thirds of the dough into a pie dish. Toss sliced apples with cinnamon, nutmeg, erythritol, and lemon zest. Place apple mixture in the crust. Crumble remaining dough on top. Bake at 350°F (177°C) for 45 mins.

N.V.: Approx. 12g net carbs per serving.

Recipe 2: Granny's Keto Apple Pie

P.T.: 1 hour

Ingr.: For the crust: 2 Cups almond flour, 1/3 Cup coconut flour, quarter Cup erythritol, half Cup butter (melted), 1 egg. For the filling: 5 green apples (sliced), half tsp cinnamon, quarter tsp ground cloves, quarter Cup water, quarter Cup erythritol, 1 tbsp chia seeds (as thickener).

Serves: 8

M.C.: Baking

Procedure: Prepare the crust by mixing all crust ingredients and pressing into a pie dish. Precook apple slices with spices, water, erythritol, and chia seeds until slightly tender. Fill the crust with the apple mixture. Use leftover dough to create a lattice top. Bake at 375°F (190°C) for 35-40 mins.

N.V.: Approx. 10g net carbs per serving.

Recipe 3: Cinnamon Swirl Apple Tart

P.T.: 1 hour 15 mins

Ingr.: For the base: 2 Cups walnut meal, quarter Cup melted butter, 1 egg. For the filling: 6 medium apples, 2 tsp cinnamon, 1/3 Cup powdered erythritol, 1 tsp vanilla extract.

Serves: 8

M.C.: Baking

Procedure: Combine walnut meal, melted butter, and egg to form a dough. Press into a tart pan. Thinly slice apples and toss with cinnamon, erythritol, and vanilla. Arrange apples over the crust. Bake at 350°F (177°C) for 50 mins.

N.V.: Approx. 9g net carbs per serving.

Recipe 4: Apple Pie in a Bowl

P.T.: 20 mins

Ingr.: 4 large apples, peeled and chopped, half tsp cinnamon, quarter tsp nutmeg, 1/8 tsp ground ginger, quarter Cup water, quarter Cup erythritol, 2 tbsp ground flaxseed (to thicken).

Serves: 4

M.C.: Stovetop

Procedure: Cook all ingredients in a saucepan over medium heat until apples are tender and the mixture has thickened (about 15 mins), stirring occasionally. Serve warm.

N.V.: Approx. 8g net carbs per serving.

Recipe 5: Mini Apple Crisp Pies

P.T.: 45 mins

Ingr.: For the crust: 1 half Cups almond flour, quarter Cup coconut oil, 1 egg. For the filling: 3 apples, 1 tsp cinnamon, quarter Cup erythritol. For the topping: half Cup chopped pecans, quarter Cup almond flour, quarter Cup shredded coconut, 2 tbsp melted coconut oil.

Serves: 6

M.C.: Baking

Procedure: Mix crust ingredients and press into mini pie pans. Mix sliced apples with cinnamon and erythritol, divide among crusts. Combine topping ingredients until crumbly; sprinkle over pies. Bake at 350°F (177°C) for 30 mins.

N.V.: Approx. 7g net carbs per serving.

3.2 Rich and Creamy Pumpkin Pie (Low-GI)

Recipe 1: Keto Pumpkin Custard Pie

P.T.: 1 hour

Ingr.: 2 Cups pumpkin puree (fresh or canned, unsweetened), 3 large eggs, 1 Cup heavy cream, half Cup erythritol, 1 tsp vanilla extract, 2 tsp pumpkin pie spice, quarter tsp salt, Almond flour pie crust (pre-baked).

Serves: 8

M.C.: Baking

Procedure: Preheat oven to 350°F (177°C). In a large bowl, whisk together pumpkin puree, eggs, heavy cream, erythritol, vanilla extract, pumpkin pie spice, and salt until smooth. Pour filling into the pre-baked almond flour crust. Bake for 45-50 mins or until the custard is set but slightly jiggly in the center. Cool completely before serving.

N.V.: Approx. 6g net carbs per serving.

Recipe 2: No-Bake Pumpkin Spice Mousse Pie

P.T.: 20 mins (plus chilling time)

Ingr.: 1 half Cups pumpkin puree, 1 Cup full-fat coconut milk (chilled overnight), half Cup erythritol, 2 tsp pumpkin pie spice, 1 tsp vanilla extract, quarter tsp salt, No-bake almond crust (almond flour, coconut oil, erythritol).

Serves: 8

M.C.: Mixing/Chilling

Procedure: Prepare the no-bake almond crust in a pie dish and chill. Whip the solid part of chilled coconut milk until creamy. Fold in pumpkin puree, erythritol, pumpkin pie spice, vanilla extract, and salt. Pour into the crust and refrigerate for at least 4 hours or until set.

N.V.: Approx. 5g net carbs per serving.

Recipe 3: Classic Pumpkin Pie with Almond Crust

P.T.: 1 hour 30 mins

Ingr.: For the crust: 2 Cups almond flour, 1/3 Cup melted butter, 1 egg. For the filling: 2 Cups pumpkin puree, 3/4 Cup almond milk, 2 eggs, half Cup erythritol, 2 tsp pumpkin pie spice, 1 tsp vanilla extract, quarter tsp salt.

Serves: 8

M.C.: Baking

Procedure: Mix almond flour, melted butter, and egg to form the crust dough. Press into a pie dish and bake at 350°F (177°C) for 10 mins. Whisk together all filling ingredients until smooth. Pour into the pre-baked crust. Bake for 50-60 mins or until the filling is set. Cool before serving.

N.V.: Approx. 7g net carbs per serving.

Recipe 4: Pumpkin Cheesecake Pie

P.T.: 1 hour 45 mins

Ingr.: 1 half Cups pumpkin puree, 1 half Cups cream cheese (softened), half Cup sour cream, half Cup erythritol, 3 eggs, 2 tsp pumpkin pie spice, 1 almond flour cheesecake crust (pre-baked).

Serves: 10

M.C.: Baking

Procedure: Beat cream cheese, pumpkin puree, sour cream, and erythritol until smooth. Add eggs one at a time, then mix in pumpkin pie spice. Pour mixture into the pre-baked cheesecake crust. Bake at 325°F (163°C) for 55-60 mins or until set. Cool and then chill before serving.

N.V.: Approx. 5g net carbs per serving.

Recipe 5: Spiced Pumpkin Pie with Coconut Crust

P.T.: 1 hour 20 mins

Ingr.: For the crust: 1 half Cups shredded unsweetened coconut, quarter Cup coconut flour, quarter Cup coconut oil, 1 egg. For the filling: 2 Cups pumpkin puree, 1 Cup coconut cream, half Cup erythritol, 3 eggs, 2 tsp pumpkin pie spice, 1 tsp vanilla extract.

Serves: 8

M.C.: Baking

Procedure: Mix shredded coconut, coconut flour, coconut oil, and egg to form the crust dough. Press into a pie dish. Bake at 350°F (177°C) for 15 mins. Whisk together pumpkin puree, coconut cream, erythritol, eggs, pumpkin pie spice, and vanilla. Pour into the crust. Bake for 45-50 mins or until the filling is set. Cool before serving.

N.V.: Approx. 8g net carbs per serving.

3.3 Summer Berry Tart (Gluten-Free)ù

Recipe 1: Almond Crust Berry Tart

P.T.: 1 hour

Ingr.: For the crust: 2 Cups almond flour, quarter Cup melted coconut oil, 1 egg. For the filling: 1 Cup mixed fresh berries (strawberries, blueberries, raspberries), 1 Cup unsweetened full-fat Greek yogurt, quarter Cup erythritol, 1 tsp vanilla extract.

Serves: 8

M.C.: Baking

Procedure: Combine almond flour, coconut oil, and egg to form the tart crust. Press into a tart pan and bake at 350°F (177°C) for 12-15 mins until golden. Cool completely. Mix Greek yogurt with erythritol and vanilla. Spread over the cooled crust. Top with fresh berries.

N.V.: Approx. 6g net carbs per serving.

Recipe 2: Coconut Flour Berry Tart

P.T.: 50 mins

Ingr.: For the crust: 1 Cup coconut flour, 1/3 Cup melted butter, 2 eggs. For the filling: 2 Cups mixed berries, half Cup heavy cream, whipped, quarter Cup powdered erythritol, 1 tsp lemon zest.

Serves: 6

M.C.: Baking

Procedure: Mix coconut flour, melted butter, and eggs to form a dough. Press into a tart pan and bake at 375°F (190°C) for 15 mins. Allow to cool. Whip heavy cream with erythritol and lemon zest until stiff peaks form. Fold in half of the berries. Spread the mixture into the crust, then top with the remaining berries.

N.V.: Approx. 8g net carbs per serving.

Recipe 3: No-Bake Berry Cashew Tart

P.T.: 2 hours (including chilling)

Ingr.: For the crust: 1 Cup cashews, 1 Cup shredded unsweetened coconut, quarter Cup coconut oil. For the filling: 1 Cup cashew cream (soaked cashews blended with water), quarter Cup erythritol, 2 Cups mixed berries, 1 tsp vanilla extract.

Serves: 8

M.C.: No-bake

Procedure: Process cashews and shredded coconut in a food processor until crumbly. Add coconut oil and blend until mixture sticks together. Press into a tart pan and chill. Mix cashew cream with erythritol and vanilla. Pour into the crust, then chill until set, about 1 hour. Top with fresh berries before serving.

N.V.: Approx. 9g net carbs per serving.

Recipe 4: Hazelnut Chocolate Berry Tart

P.T.: 1 hour 30 mins

Ingr.: For the crust: 2 Cups ground hazelnuts, quarter Cup cocoa powder, quarter Cup melted butter. For the filling: 1 Cup mixed berries, 1 Cup mascarpone cheese, quarter Cup powdered erythritol, 1 tsp vanilla extract.

Serves: 8

M.C.: Baking

Procedure: Combine ground hazelnuts, cocoa powder, and melted butter. Press into a tart pan and bake at 350°F (177°C) for 18-20 mins. Cool. Mix mascarpone with erythritol and vanilla until smooth. Spread over the cooled crust. Top with berries.

N.V.: Approx. 7g net carbs per serving.

Recipe 5: Lemon Berry Flaxseed Tart

P.T.: 1 hour

Ingr.: For the crust: 1.5 Cups flaxseed meal, quarter Cup coconut oil, 1 egg. For the filling: 2 Cups mixed berries, 1 Cup unsweetened Greek yogurt, quarter Cup erythritol, zest of 1 lemon.

Serves: 8

M.C.: Baking

Procedure: Mix flaxseed meal, coconut oil, and egg to form the crust. Press into a tart pan and bake at 350°F (177°C) for 15 mins. Cool. Mix Greek yogurt with erythritol and lemon zest. Spread onto the crust. Arrange berries on top.

N.V.: Approx. 5g net carbs per serving.

Chapter 4: Cookies and Biscotti

4.1 Almond Flour Chocolate Chip Cookies

Recipe 1: Classic Almond Joy Cookies

P.T.: 25 mins

Ingr.: 2 Cups almond flour, half Cup coconut oil (melted), quarter Cup erythritol, 1 large egg, 1 tsp vanilla extract, half tsp baking soda, quarter tsp salt, half Cup sugar-free chocolate chips.

Serves: 12

M.C.: Baking

Procedure: Preheat the oven to 350°F (177°C). In a bowl, mix almond flour, baking soda, and salt. In another bowl, whisk melted coconut oil, erythritol, egg, and vanilla. Combine wet and dry ingredients, then fold in chocolate chips. Drop spoonfuls onto a baking sheet and bake for 10-12 mins until edges are golden. Cool on a wire rack.

N.V.: Approx. 2g net carbs per cookie.

Recipe 2: Cocoa Chip Almond Bites

P.T.: 30 mins

Ingr.: 1.5 Cups almond flour, quarter Cup unsweetened cocoa powder, 1/3 Cup melted butter, 1/3 Cup erythritol, 1 egg, 1 tsp vanilla extract, half tsp baking powder, quarter tsp salt, half Cup sugar-free chocolate chips.

Serves: 15

M.C.: Baking

Procedure: Preheat oven to 375°F (190°C). Combine almond flour, cocoa powder, baking powder, and salt. In a separate bowl, mix melted butter, erythritol, egg, and vanilla. Merge wet and dry ingredients, then stir in chocolate chips. Scoop onto a parchment-lined baking sheet. Bake for 12-15 mins. Let cool.

N.V.: Approx. 3g net carbs per cookie.

Recipe 3: Almond Butter Choc-Chip Delights

P.T.: 20 mins

Ingr.: 2 Cups almond flour, half Cup almond butter, quarter Cup erythritol, 1 egg, half tsp baking soda, quarter tsp salt, 1 tsp vanilla extract, half Cup sugar-free chocolate chips.

Serves: 12

M.C.: Baking

Procedure: Mix almond flour, baking soda, and salt. In another bowl, blend almond butter, erythritol, egg, and vanilla. Combine both mixtures, then fold in chocolate chips. Spoon dough onto a baking sheet. Bake at 350°F (177°C) for 8-10 mins. Cool before serving.

N.V.: Approx. 1.5g net carbs per cookie.

Recipe 4: Vanilla Chocolate Chunk Cookies

P.T.: 35 mins

Ingr.: 2 Cups almond flour, 1/3 Cup coconut oil (solid), 1/3 Cup erythritol, 1 large egg, 2 tsp vanilla extract, half tsp baking soda, half tsp salt, 3/4 Cup sugar-free dark chocolate, chopped.

Serves: 16

M.C.: Baking

Procedure: Preheat oven to 350°F (177°C). Whisk together almond flour, baking soda, and salt. Cream coconut oil and erythritol until fluffy. Add egg and vanilla, mix well. Gradually add dry ingredients. Stir in chopped chocolate. Place dough balls on baking sheet, flatten slightly. Bake for 13-15 mins. Transfer to wire rack to cool.

N.V.: Approx. 2g net carbs per cookie.

Recipe 5: Nutty Chocolate Chip Almond Cookies

P.T.: 28 mins

Ingr.: 2.5 Cups almond flour, quarter Cup grass-fed butter (melted), quarter Cup erythritol, 1 egg, 1 tsp almond extract, half tsp baking soda, quarter tsp salt, half Cup sugar-free chocolate chips, half Cup chopped walnuts.

Serves: 18

M.C.: Baking

Procedure: Preheat the oven to 375°F (190°C). Mix almond flour, baking soda, and salt. In another bowl, combine melted butter, erythritol, egg, and almond extract. Fold wet ingredients into dry, then add chocolate chips and walnuts. Scoop onto a lined baking sheet, bake for 10-12 mins. Let them cool on the sheet before moving to a cooling rack.

N.V.: Approx. 2g net carbs per cookie.

4.2 Crunchy Pistachio Biscotti (Sugar-Free)

Recipe 1: Classic Pistachio Almond Biscotti

P.T.: 55 mins

Ingr.: 2 Cups almond flour, half Cup erythritol, 1 tsp baking powder, quarter tsp salt, 3 large eggs, 1 tsp vanilla extract, 1 Cup chopped pistachios.

Serves: 12

M.C.: Baking

Procedure: Preheat oven to 350°F (177°C). Mix almond flour, erythritol, baking powder, and salt. In a separate bowl, whisk eggs and vanilla. Combine wet and dry ingredients, then fold in pistachios. Form a log on a parchment-lined baking sheet. Bake for 25 mins, cool slightly, slice, and bake again for 15 mins.

N.V.: Approx. 2g net carbs per biscotti.

Recipe 2: Lemon Zest Pistachio Biscotti

P.T.: 1 hour

Ingr.: 2 Cups almond flour, quarter Cup powdered erythritol, 1 tsp baking powder, half tsp salt, zest of 1 lemon, 2 eggs, 1 tsp lemon extract, 1 Cup pistachios (whole).

Serves: 10

M.C.: Baking

Procedure: Combine almond flour, erythritol, baking powder, salt, and lemon zest. Beat eggs and lemon extract, then mix into dry ingredients. Stir in pistachios. Shape dough into a log on a baking sheet. Bake at 325°F (163°C) for 30 mins, then slice and bake again for 20 mins.

N.V.: Approx. 3g net carbs per serving.

Recipe 3: Chocolate Dipped Pistachio Biscotti

P.T.: 1 hour 10 mins

Ingr.: 2.5 Cups almond flour, 1/3 Cup erythritol, 1 tsp baking powder, 2 eggs, 1 tsp vanilla extract, 1 Cup chopped pistachios, half Cup sugar-free dark chocolate (melted).

Serves: 12

M.C.: Baking

Procedure: Preheat oven to 350°F (177°C). Mix almond flour, erythritol, and baking powder. Blend in eggs and vanilla, then fold in pistachios. Form dough into a log, bake for 30 mins, cool, slice, and bake slices for 20 mins. Dip in melted chocolate.

N.V.: Approx. 4g net carbs per biscotti.

Recipe 4: Orange Pistachio Biscotti

P.T.: 1 hour

Ingr.: 2 Cups almond flour, half Cup granulated erythritol, 1 tsp baking powder, quarter tsp salt, zest of 1 orange, 2 large eggs, half tsp almond extract, 1 Cup pistachios (chopped).

Serves: 15

M.C.: Baking

Procedure: Preheat oven to 325°F (163°C). Combine almond flour, erythritol, baking powder, salt, and orange zest. Whisk eggs and almond extract together and add to dry ingredients. Stir in chopped pistachios. Shape into a log, bake, then slice and bake slices until crisp.

N.V.: Approx. 2g net carbs per biscotti.

Recipe 5: Espresso Pistachio Biscotti

P.T.: 1 hour 15 mins

Ingr.: 2 Cups almond flour, 1/3 Cup erythritol, 1 tsp baking powder, quarter tsp salt, 2 tsp instant espresso powder, 2 eggs, 1 tsp vanilla extract, 1 Cup pistachios.

Serves: 12

M.C.: Baking

Procedure: Mix almond flour, erythritol, baking powder, salt, and espresso powder. Beat in eggs and vanilla. Fold in pistachios. Form a dough log on a baking sheet. Bake at 350°F (177°C) for 25 mins, cool, slice, and bake slices for an additional 20 mins.

N.V.: Approx. 3g net carbs per biscotti.

4.3 Oatmeal Raisin Cookies (Sweetened with Dates)

Recipe 1: Date-Sweetened Oatmeal Delights

P.T.: 35 mins

Ingr.: 1 Cup pitted dates, soaked and pureed, 2 Cups rolled oats, half Cup almond flour, 1 tsp cinnamon, half tsp baking soda, quarter tsp salt, 2 eggs, 1 tsp vanilla extract, half Cup raisins, quarter Cup chopped walnuts.

Serves: 12

M.C.: Baking

Procedure: Preheat oven to 350°F (177°C). Mix oats, almond flour, cinnamon, baking soda, and salt. Stir in date puree, eggs, and vanilla until well combined. Fold in raisins and walnuts. Spoon onto a baking sheet and bake for 15-18 mins.

N.V.: Since specifics are requested to be omitted, please note these are naturally sweetened and healthier.

Recipe 2: Nutty Date Oat Cookies

P.T.: 40 mins

Ingr.: 1 Cup finely chopped dates, 1 Cup quick oats, half Cup ground flaxseed, 1 tsp cinnamon, quarter Cup unsweetened applesauce, 1 egg, half tsp vanilla extract, 1/3 Cup chopped pecans, 1/3 Cup raisins.

Serves: 10

M.C.: Baking

Procedure: Combine dates, oats, flaxseed, and cinnamon. Mix in applesauce, egg, and vanilla. Stir in pecans and raisins. Drop spoonfuls on a lined baking tray. Bake at 325°F (163°C) for 20-25 mins.

N.V.: Emphasizes natural ingredients for a healthier alternative.

Recipe 3: Date-Sweetened Cinnamon Raisin Cookies

P.T.: 30 mins

Ingr.: 1 half Cups rolled oats, 3/4 Cup date paste (from soaked, blended dates), half Cup raisins, 2 tsp cinnamon, 1 egg, quarter Cup melted coconut oil, 1 tsp baking powder, quarter tsp salt, half tsp vanilla extract.

Serves: 12

M.C.: Baking

Procedure: Mix oats, cinnamon, baking powder, and salt. Add date paste, egg, coconut oil, and vanilla. Combine thoroughly before folding in raisins. Spoon onto a baking sheet, flattening slightly. Bake at 350°F (177°C) for 12-15 mins.

N.V.: Features a blend of natural sweetness and spices.

Recipe 4: Simple Date Oatmeal Cookies

P.T.: 25 mins

Ingr.: 1 Cup rolled oats, 1 Cup date puree, 1 egg, 1 tsp vanilla extract, half tsp baking soda, half Cup raisins, quarter tsp salt, half tsp cinnamon.

Serves: 8

M.C.: Baking

Procedure: Combine all ingredients except raisins in a large bowl. Once mixed, fold in raisins. Drop by spoonfuls onto a parchment-lined baking sheet. Bake at 375°F (190°C) for 10-12 mins.

N.V.: Crafted for those seeking simplicity and natural sweetness.

Recipe 5: Spiced Date and Oat Cookies

P.T.: 45 mins

Ingr.: 2 Cups rolled oats, 1 Cup soaked and pureed dates, quarter Cup almond milk, 1 tsp ground ginger, 1 tsp cinnamon, half tsp nutmeg, 1 egg, half tsp vanilla extract, half Cup raisins, quarter tsp baking soda.

Serves: 14

M.C.: Baking

Procedure: Preheat oven to 350°F (177°C). Stir together oats, spices, and baking soda. In another bowl, combine date puree, almond milk, egg, and vanilla. Mix wet ingredients into dry

until combined, then fold in raisins. Drop by spoonfuls onto a baking sheet and bake for 15 mins.
N.V.: Aromatic spices complement the natural sweetness, offering a rich flavor profile.

Chapter 5: Brownies and Bars

5.1 Fudgy Avocado Brownies (Low-Carb)

Recipe 1: Classic Avocado Cocoa Brownies

P.T.: 35 mins

Ingr.: 2 ripe avocados, mashed; 3 eggs; half Cup almond flour; half Cup unsweetened cocoa powder; quarter Cup erythritol; 1 tsp vanilla extract; half tsp baking soda; quarter tsp salt; half Cup sugar-free dark chocolate chips.

Serves: 12

M.C.: Baking

Procedure: Preheat the oven to 350°F (177°C). Mix mashed avocados, eggs, and vanilla extract until smooth. Combine almond flour, cocoa powder, erythritol, baking soda, and salt in another bowl. Gradually mix dry ingredients into wet ingredients until well blended. Fold in chocolate chips. Pour into a greased 8x8 inch baking pan. Bake for 25 mins. Cool before cutting into squares.

N.V.: Rich in healthy fats with minimal net carbs.

Recipe 2: Avocado Espresso Brownies

P.T.: 40 mins

Ingr.: 1 large ripe avocado, pureed; 3 eggs; quarter Cup almond flour; 3/4 Cup unsweetened cocoa powder; 1/3 Cup erythritol; 2 tsp espresso powder; 1 tsp baking powder; half tsp salt; 1 tsp vanilla extract; quarter Cup unsweetened almond milk; half Cup sugar-free dark chocolate chunks.

Serves: 10

M.C.: Baking

Procedure: Blend avocado, eggs, vanilla extract, and almond milk. Mix almond flour, cocoa powder, erythritol, espresso powder, baking powder, and salt in a separate bowl. Combine wet and dry ingredients, then stir in chocolate chunks. Bake in a preheated 350°F (177°C) oven in a lined 9x9 inch pan for 30 mins. Let cool before slicing.

N.V.: Offers a caffeine kick with low net carbs.

Recipe 3: Nutty Avocado Brownies

P.T.: 45 mins

Ingr.: 2 avocados, mashed; 2 eggs; half Cup coconut flour; half Cup unsweetened cocoa powder; quarter Cup granulated monk fruit sweetener; 1 tsp vanilla extract; half tsp baking soda; quarter Cup melted coconut oil; quarter tsp sea salt; half Cup chopped walnuts.

Serves: 12

M.C.: Baking

Procedure: Whisk together mashed avocados, eggs, vanilla, and coconut oil. Stir in coconut flour, cocoa powder, monk fruit sweetener, baking soda, and salt until smooth. Fold in walnuts. Spread batter in a prepared 8x8 inch baking dish. Bake at 350°F (177°C) for 35 mins. Cool before serving.

N.V.: Packed with fiber and healthy fats, very low in net carbs.

Recipe 4: Avocado Mint Chocolate Brownies

P.T.: 50 mins

Ingr.: 2 medium avocados, pureed; 3 eggs; half Cup almond flour; half Cup unsweetened cocoa powder; 1/3 Cup erythritol; half tsp baking powder; quarter tsp salt; 1 tsp mint extract; half Cup sugar-free chocolate chips; fresh mint leaves for garnish.

Serves: 12

M.C.: Baking

Procedure: Combine avocado puree, eggs, and mint extract. In another bowl, mix almond flour, cocoa powder, erythritol, baking powder, and salt. Merge the mixtures and fold in chocolate chips. Pour into a greased 9x9 inch pan. Bake at 350°F (177°C) for 25-30 mins. Garnish with mint leaves after cooling.

N.V.: Low-carb, enriched with the freshness of mint.

Recipe 5: Spicy Avocado Chocolate Brownies

P.T.: 38 mins

Ingr.: 2 ripe avocados, mashed; 4 eggs; quarter Cup coconut flour; 3/4 Cup unsweetened cocoa powder; half Cup erythritol; 1 tsp vanilla extract; half tsp cinnamon; quarter tsp cayenne pepper; half tsp baking soda; quarter tsp salt; half Cup sugar-free chocolate chips.

Serves: 12

M.C.: Baking

Procedure: Mix avocados, eggs, and vanilla. Combine coconut flour, cocoa powder, erythritol, cinnamon, cayenne, baking soda, and salt in another bowl. Blend dry ingredients into wet, then stir in chocolate chips. Spread in a greased 8x8 inch pan. Bake at 350°F (177°C) for 20-25 mins. Allow to cool before cutting.

N.V.: Low-carb with a spicy kick, perfect for those seeking a unique flavor profile.

5.2 Raspberry Oat Bars (No Added Sugar)

Recipe 1: Raspberry Chia Oat Bars

P.T.: 45 mins

Ingr.: 2 Cups rolled oats, 1 Cup unsweetened applesauce, half Cup chia seeds, 1 tsp vanilla extract, 2 Cups fresh raspberries, quarter Cup crushed walnuts, quarter Cup unsweetened shredded coconut.

Serves: 12

M.C.: Baking

Procedure: Preheat oven to 350°F (177°C). Mix oats, applesauce, chia seeds, and vanilla in a bowl. Press half of the mixture into a lined 8x8 baking dish. Layer raspberries over the base. Sprinkle with walnuts and coconut, then top with the remaining oat mixture. Bake for 30 mins until golden. Cool before cutting into bars.

N.V.: High in fiber and omega-3 fatty acids, with natural sweetness.

Recipe 2: Nutty Raspberry Oat Squares

P.T.: 50 mins

Ingr.: 1.5 Cups rolled oats, 1 Cup almond flour, half Cup crushed almonds, 1/3 Cup melted coconut oil, 2 Cups raspberries (fresh or frozen), 2 tbsp lemon juice, 1 tbsp lemon zest, half Cup water, half tsp cinnamon.

Serves: 10

M.C.: Baking

Procedure: Combine oats, almond flour, almonds, and cinnamon. Mix in coconut oil. Press 3/4 of the mixture into a greased 9x9 inch pan. Simmer raspberries, lemon juice, zest, and water until thickened. Spread over the oat base. Crumble remaining oat mixture on top. Bake at 375°F (190°C) for 35 mins. Cool before slicing.

N.V.: Rich in healthy fats and antioxidants, minimal natural sugars.

Recipe 3: Raspberry Oatmeal Breakfast Bars

P.T.: 40 mins

Ingr.: 2 Cups rolled oats, 1 Cup raspberries, 1 ripe banana, mashed, quarter Cup almond butter, quarter Cup flaxseed meal, 1 tsp cinnamon, half Cup unsweetened almond milk, 1 tsp vanilla extract.

Serves: 8

M.C.: Baking

Procedure: Preheat oven to 350°F (177°C). In a large bowl, combine oats, flaxseed, and cinnamon. Mix in mashed banana, almond butter, almond milk, and vanilla until well blended. Fold in raspberries gently. Press mixture into a lined 8x8 inch baking dish. Bake for 25-30 mins. Allow to cool before cutting.

N.V.: High in dietary fiber, with natural fruit sweetness.

Recipe 4: Lemon Raspberry Oat Crumble Bars

P.T.: 55 mins

Ingr.: 2 Cups rolled oats, 1 Cup unsweetened dried coconut flakes, half Cup almond slices, quarter Cup coconut oil, melted, 2 Cups raspberries, 1 tbsp grated lemon zest, quarter Cup fresh lemon juice, quarter Cup water, 2 tbsp chia seeds.

Serves: 12

M.C.: Baking

Procedure: Stir together oats, coconut flakes, almond slices, and lemon zest. Add melted coconut oil to the oat mixture until crumbly. Press half into a lined baking dish. Cook raspberries, lemon juice, water, and chia seeds over medium heat until jammy. Spread raspberry layer over the oat base. Top with remaining oat mixture. Bake at 375°F (190°C) for 25 mins. Cool completely.

N.V.: Offers a good balance of tartness and sweetness, high in vitamin C and fiber.

5.3 Peanut Butter Swirl Chocolate Bars (Keto-Friendly)

Recipe 1: Decadent Keto Peanut Butter Swirl Bars

P.T.: 1 hour

Ingr.: 2 Cups sugar-free dark chocolate chips, 1 Cup creamy natural peanut butter (unsweetened), half Cup coconut oil, quarter Cup powdered erythritol, 1 tsp vanilla extract, 1 pinch of salt.

Serves: 12

M.C.: Melting/Freezing

Procedure: Melt chocolate chips with coconut oil and a pinch of salt over low heat until smooth. Pour half into a parchment-lined baking dish, freezing for 10 mins. Mix peanut butter, erythritol, and vanilla, then gently spread over the set chocolate layer. Top with remaining chocolate mixture, swirling with a knife. Freeze until solid. Slice into bars.

N.V.: High in fats, low in net carbs, making it perfectly keto-friendly.

Recipe 2: Keto Peanut Butter Chocolate Dream Bars

P.T.: 2 hours

Ingr.: For the base - 1.5 Cups almond flour, quarter Cup cocoa powder, 1/3 Cup melted butter; For the filling - 1 Cup unsweetened peanut butter, half Cup coconut cream, 1/3 Cup powdered erythritol; For the topping - 1 Cup sugar-free chocolate chips, 2 tbsp coconut oil.

Serves: 12

M.C.: Baking/Chilling

Procedure: Combine almond flour and cocoa with melted butter, press into a pan, and bake at 350°F (177°C) for 15 mins. Cool. Blend peanut butter, coconut cream, and erythritol, then spread over the crust. Melt chocolate chips with coconut oil, pour over the peanut butter layer. Chill for 1-2 hours.

N.V.: Primarily fats, minimal net carbs.

Recipe 3: Swirled Peanut Butter Keto Bars

P.T.: 45 mins

Ingr.: 2 Cups sugar-free chocolate chips, 1 Cup smooth peanut butter (no added sugar), quarter Cup heavy cream, quarter Cup powdered erythritol, half tsp sea salt, 1 tsp vanilla extract.

Serves: 10

M.C.: Melting/Refrigerating

Procedure: Melt chocolate chips gently, stir in heavy cream and vanilla until smooth. In another bowl, mix peanut butter with erythritol and salt. Pour chocolate mixture into a silicone mold or lined tray, add dollops of peanut butter mixture, and swirl with a toothpick. Refrigerate until set, then cut into bars.

N.V.: Contains healthy fats, extremely low in carbs.

Recipe 4: Nutty Chocolate Peanut Butter Keto Squares

P.T.: 1 hour 30 mins

Ingr.: For the chocolate layer - 1.5 Cups sugar-free chocolate chips, quarter Cup unsalted butter; For the peanut butter layer - 1 Cup creamy peanut butter (unsweetened), quarter Cup coconut oil, quarter Cup powdered erythritol, half tsp vanilla extract.

Serves: 16

M.C.: Layering/Freezing

Procedure: Melt chocolate chips and butter, spread into a parchment-lined tray, and freeze for 20 mins. Heat peanut butter and coconut oil until smooth, remove from heat, mix in erythritol and vanilla. Pour over the chocolate layer, freeze until set. Slice into squares.

N.V.: Predominantly fats, suitable for a keto diet with very low net carbs.

Chapter 6: Muffins and Cupcakes

6.1 Blueberry Muffins (Sugar-Free)

Recipe 1: Classic Keto Blueberry Muffins

P.T.: 30 mins

Ingr.: 2 Cups almond flour, 1/3 Cup erythritol, 1 tsp baking powder, half tsp baking soda, quarter tsp salt, 3 large eggs, quarter Cup unsweetened almond milk, quarter Cup melted unsalted butter, 1 tsp vanilla extract, 1 Cup fresh blueberries.

Serves: 12

M.C.: Baking

Procedure: Preheat the oven to 350°F (177°C). Whisk together almond flour, erythritol, baking powder, baking soda, and salt. In another bowl, beat eggs, almond milk, melted butter, and vanilla extract. Combine wet and dry ingredients, gently fold in blueberries. Distribute batter into muffin Cups and bake for 20-25 mins.

N.V.: Primarily fats, minimal net carbs.

Recipe 2: Lemon Zest Blueberry Muffins

P.T.: 35 mins

Ingr.: 2 Cups almond flour, quarter Cup granulated monk fruit sweetener, 1 tsp baking powder, 3 eggs, half Cup coconut oil (melted), zest of 1 lemon, 1 tsp lemon extract, 1 Cup blueberries (fresh or frozen, unsweetened).

Serves: 10

M.C.: Baking

Procedure: Mix almond flour, monk fruit sweetener, and baking powder. In a separate bowl, combine eggs, melted coconut oil, lemon zest, and lemon extract. Mix wet ingredients into dry, then fold in blueberries. Spoon into muffin tins and bake at 350°F (177°C) for about 22 mins.

N.V.: Low in net carbs, rich in healthy fats.

Recipe 3: Nutty Blueberry Muffins

P.T.: 40 mins

Ingr.: 1.5 Cups almond flour, half Cup crushed walnuts, 1/3 Cup erythritol, 1 tsp baking powder, quarter Cup unsalted butter (melted), 2 eggs, half tsp vanilla extract, half Cup unsweetened almond milk, 1 Cup blueberries.

Serves: 12

M.C.: Baking

Procedure: Combine almond flour, walnuts, erythritol, and baking powder. Whisk together melted butter, eggs, vanilla extract, and almond milk. Stir wet ingredients into dry, then gently mix in blueberries. Pour batter into muffin Cups and bake at 375°F (190°C) for 25 mins.

N.V.: High in protein and fiber, with very low net carbs.

Recipe 4: Cinnamon Swirl Blueberry Muffins

P.T.: 45 mins

Ingr.: 2 Cups almond flour, quarter Cup erythritol, 1 tbsp ground cinnamon, 1 tsp baking powder, quarter tsp salt, 3 large eggs, 1/3 Cup melted coconut oil, quarter Cup unsweetened almond milk, 1 tsp vanilla extract, 1 Cup blueberries.

Serves: 10

M.C.: Baking

Procedure: Preheat oven to 350°F (177°C). Mix almond flour, erythritol, cinnamon, baking powder, and salt. In a separate bowl, blend eggs, coconut oil, almond milk, and vanilla. Combine with dry ingredients, fold in blueberries. Fill muffin tins, sprinkle with a mix of erythritol and cinnamon. Bake for 20 mins.

N.V.: Offers a balance of flavors with negligible net carbs.

6.2 Carrot Cake Cupcakes (With Cream Cheese Frosting)

Recipe 1: Keto Carrot-Infused Cupcakes

P.T.: 45 mins

Ingr.: For Cupcakes - 2 Cups almond flour, half Cup grated carrots, 1/3 Cup erythritol, 2 tsp cinnamon, 1 tsp nutmeg, 1 tsp baking powder, 4 eggs, quarter Cup unsweetened almond milk, quarter Cup coconut oil. For frosting - 1 Cup cream cheese, quarter Cup butter (softened), quarter Cup powdered erythritol, 1 tsp vanilla extract.

Serves: 12

M.C.: Baking

Procedure: Mix almond flour, erythritol, spices, and baking powder. Incorporate eggs, almond milk, and coconut oil. Fold in carrots. Divide into muffin tins, bake at 350°F (177°C) for 20 mins. For frosting, beat cream cheese, butter, erythritol, and vanilla until smooth. Frost cooled Cupcakes.

N.V.: High in healthy fats, low in net carbs.

Recipe 2: Spiced Carrot Almond Cupcakes

P.T.: 50 mins

Ingr.: For Cupcakes - 1.5 Cups almond flour, quarter Cup coconut flour, half Cup grated carrots, 1/3 Cup granulated monk fruit sweetener, 2 tsp cinnamon, half tsp ginger, quarter tsp cloves, 3 eggs, 1/3 Cup coconut oil, 1 tsp vanilla. For frosting - 8 oz cream cheese, 3 tbsp powdered monk fruit sweetener, 1 tsp lemon zest.

Serves: 12

M.C.: Baking

Procedure: Combine dry ingredients. Mix in eggs, oil, and vanilla. Stir in carrots. Bake in lined Cups at 325°F (163°C) for 23 mins. Blend frosting ingredients, apply to cooled Cupcakes.

N.V.: Minimal net carbs, suitable for keto.

Recipe 3: Nutty Carrot Cake Minis

P.T.: 55 mins

Ingr.: For Cupcakes - 2 Cups almond flour, half Cup finely chopped walnuts, half Cup shredded carrots, 1/3 Cup erythritol, 2 tsp baking powder, 1 tsp cinnamon, 4 eggs, half Cup melted butter. For frosting - 1 Cup cream cheese, quarter Cup erythritol, half tsp vanilla extract, quarter Cup chopped pecans for topping.

Serves: 12

M.C.: Baking

Procedure: Mix almond flour, walnuts, erythritol, baking powder, and cinnamon. Add eggs and butter. Fold in carrots. Spoon into Cupcake molds, bake at 350°F (177°C) for 25 mins. Mix frosting ingredients, chill. Frost Cupcakes, sprinkle pecans.

N.V.: Low in carbs, rich in proteins and healthy fats.

Recipe 4: Classic Keto Carrot Cupcakes

P.T.: 1 hour

Ingr.: For Cupcakes - 2 Cups almond flour, quarter Cup flaxseed meal, half Cup grated carrots, quarter Cup erythritol, 2 tsp cinnamon, 1 tsp allspice, 1 tsp baking powder, 3 eggs, quarter Cup heavy cream, quarter Cup olive oil. For frosting - 8 oz cream cheese, quarter Cup softened butter, quarter Cup powdered erythritol, 1 tsp almond extract.

Serves: 12

M.C.: Baking

Procedure: Whisk together almond flour, flaxseed meal, erythritol, spices, and baking powder. Beat in eggs, heavy cream, and oil. Stir in carrots. Fill Cupcake liners, bake at 350°F (177°C) for 22 mins. For frosting, beat cream cheese, butter, erythritol, and almond extract until fluffy. Frost cooled Cupcakes.

N.V.: High in fiber and healthy fats, very low net carbs.

6.3 Zucchini Chocolate Chip Muffins (Low-Carb)

Recipe 1: Keto Zucchini Cocoa Nib Muffins

P.T.: 35 mins

Ingr.: 2 Cups almond flour, half Cup cocoa powder, 1/3 Cup erythritol, 1 tsp baking powder, quarter tsp salt, 3 eggs, 1 Cup grated zucchini (excess moisture squeezed out), half Cup unsweetened almond milk, quarter Cup melted coconut oil, 1 tsp vanilla extract, half Cup cocoa nibs.

Serves: 12

M.C.: Baking

Procedure: Mix almond flour, cocoa powder, erythritol, baking powder, and salt. Whisk in eggs, almond milk, coconut oil, and vanilla. Fold in zucchini and cocoa nibs. Spoon into muffin tins and bake at 350°F (177°C) for 20 mins.

N.V.: Primarily fats, minimal net carbs, rich in fiber.

Recipe 2: Zucchini Almond Chocolate Chip Muffins

P.T.: 40 mins

Ingr.: 2 Cups almond flour, quarter Cup granulated monk fruit sweetener, 1 tsp baking soda, half tsp cinnamon, 3 eggs, 1 Cup shredded zucchini, quarter Cup olive oil, 1 tsp apple cider vinegar, half Cup sugar-free chocolate chips.

Serves: 12

M.C.: Baking

Procedure: Combine almond flour, monk fruit sweetener, baking soda, and cinnamon. Beat eggs, then mix in zucchini, oil, and vinegar. Combine with dry ingredients, stir in chocolate chips. Distribute into muffin Cups, bake at 350°F (177°C) for 25 mins.

N.V.: High in healthy fats, low in carbs.

Recipe 3: Coconut Zucchini Chocolate Muffins

P.T.: 45 mins

Ingr.: 1.5 Cups coconut flour, 1/3 Cup erythritol, 1 tsp baking powder, half tsp salt, 4 eggs, 1 Cup grated zucchini, half Cup coconut cream, quarter Cup melted butter, 1 tsp vanilla extract, half Cup sugar-free chocolate chips.

Serves: 10

M.C.: Baking

Procedure: Stir together coconut flour, erythritol, baking powder, and salt. Whisk eggs, coconut cream, butter, and vanilla. Mix into dry ingredients, fold in zucchini and chocolate chips. Spoon into muffin pans, bake at 375°F (190°C) for 22 mins.

N.V.: Low in net carbs, high in dietary fiber.

Recipe 4: Zucchini Walnut Chocolate Muffins

P.T.: 50 mins

Ingr.: 2 Cups almond flour, quarter Cup powdered erythritol, 1 tsp baking soda, quarter tsp nutmeg, 4 eggs, 1 Cup finely grated zucchini, 1/3 Cup coconut oil, 1 tsp vanilla extract, half Cup chopped walnuts, half Cup sugar-free chocolate chips.

Serves: 12

M.C.: Baking

Procedure: Mix almond flour, erythritol, baking soda, and nutmeg. In another bowl, whisk eggs, zucchini, oil, and vanilla. Combine wet and dry mixtures, then fold in walnuts and chocolate chips. Fill muffin Cups, bake at 350°F (177°C) for 25-30 mins.

N.V.: Nutrient-rich, with essential fatty acids and low in carbs.

Chapter 7: Frozen Desserts

7.1 Strawberry Frozen Yogurt (No-Sugar-Added)

Recipe 1: Classic Creamy Strawberry Frozen Yogurt

P.T.: 4 hours 15 mins

Ingr.: 3 Cups fresh strawberries, hulled; 2 Cups plain Greek yogurt (full-fat for creaminess); 1/3 Cup erythritol; 1 tsp vanilla extract; juice of half lemon.

Serves: 4

M.C.: Blending/Freezing

Procedure: Puree strawberries in a blender until smooth. Add Greek yogurt, erythritol, vanilla extract, and lemon juice, blending until well combined. Pour the mixture into an ice cream maker and churn according to the manufacturer's instructions, or freeze in a container, stirring every hour to break up ice crystals, until firm yet creamy.

N.V.: Rich in protein, virtually no added sugars.

Recipe 2: Strawberry Basil Frozen Yogurt

P.T.: 4 hours 20 mins

Ingr.: 3 Cups strawberries, quartered; 2 Cups plain Greek yogurt; quarter Cup fresh basil leaves, chopped; quarter Cup erythritol; 1 tbsp lemon zest.

Serves: 4

M.C.: Blending/Freezing

Procedure: Combine strawberries, basil, erythritol, and lemon zest in a food processor, pulse until strawberries are coarsely chopped. Mix in Greek yogurt until just combined. Transfer to an ice cream maker and churn, or freeze in a shallow dish, stirring occasionally. Serve when ready.

N.V.: High in antioxidants, no added sugars.

Recipe 3: Strawberry Coconut Frozen Yogurt

P.T.: 4 hours 10 mins

Ingr.: 2 Cups strawberries, hulled and halved; 2 Cups coconut Greek yogurt; 1/3 Cup powdered erythritol; 1 tsp vanilla extract; half Cup unsweetened coconut flakes.

Serves: 6

M.C.: Blending/Freezing

Procedure: Puree strawberries until smooth. Blend with coconut Greek yogurt, erythritol, and vanilla. Fold in coconut flakes. Pour into a freezing container or follow ice cream maker instructions. Freeze until set, stirring as needed.

N.V.: Low in carbs, enhanced with coconut's healthy fats.

Recipe 4: Minty Strawberry Frozen Yogurt

P.T.: 4 hours 5 mins

Ingr.: 3 Cups strawberries; 2 Cups plain Greek yogurt; quarter Cup erythritol; 2 tsp fresh mint, finely chopped; 1 tsp lemon juice.

Serves: 5

M.C.: Blending/Freezing

Procedure: In a blender, combine strawberries, Greek yogurt, erythritol, mint, and lemon juice until smooth. If using an ice cream maker, churn according to instructions. Otherwise, freeze in a container, stirring occasionally to maintain a creamy texture. Serve once firm.

N.V.: Offers a refreshing twist with virtually no added sugars and low carbs.

7.2 Chocolate Peanut Butter Ice Cream (Low-Carb)

Recipe 1: Keto Double Chocolate Peanut Butter Swirl

P.T.: 6 hours

Ingr.: 2 Cups heavy cream, 1 Cup unsweetened almond milk, 1/3 Cup unsweetened cocoa powder, half Cup powdered erythritol, 1 tsp vanilla extract, half Cup unsweetened peanut butter, quarter Cup sugar-free dark chocolate chips.

Serves: 8

M.C.: Freezing

Procedure: Whisk together cream, almond milk, cocoa powder, erythritol, and vanilla in a large bowl until smooth. Pour mixture into an ice cream maker and churn according to manufacturer's instructions. Five mins before it's done, add peanut butter in dollops and chocolate chips. Transfer to a freezer-safe container and freeze until firm.

N.V.: High in fats, low in net carbs, making it perfectly keto-friendly.

Recipe 2: Peanut Butter Fudge Ripple Ice Cream

P.T.: 5 hours

Ingr.: 2 Cups heavy cream, 1 Cup coconut milk (full-fat), quarter Cup unsweetened cocoa powder, half Cup powdered erythritol, 2 tsp vanilla extract, 1/3 Cup natural peanut butter, 1 tbsp coconut oil.

Serves: 6

M.C.: Mixing/Freezing

Procedure: Mix cream, coconut milk, cocoa powder, erythritol, and vanilla in a blender until smooth. Freeze using an ice cream maker. Separately, melt peanut butter with coconut oil until pourable. Swirl into the ice cream during the last few mins of churning. Freeze until ready to serve.

N.V.: Rich in healthy fats and very low in carbohydrates.

Recipe 3: No-Churn Chocolate Peanut Butter Delight

P.T.: 6 hours 15 mins

Ingr.: 2 Cups whipped cream, 1 Cup unsweetened almond milk, 1/3 Cup unsweetened cocoa powder, quarter Cup erythritol, 1 tsp vanilla extract, half Cup creamy peanut butter.

Serves: 8

M.C.: Whipping/Freezing

Procedure: Whip the cream to stiff peaks. In another bowl, mix almond milk, cocoa powder, erythritol, and vanilla. Fold this mixture into the whipped cream gently. Swirl in peanut butter. Freeze in a container for at least 6 hours.

N.V.: Minimal net carbs, high in dietary fat.

Recipe 4: Creamy Peanut Butter Cocoa Ice Cream

P.T.: 5 hours 30 mins

Ingr.: 1.5 Cups heavy cream, 3/4 Cup unsweetened almond milk, half Cup unsweetened cocoa powder, 1/3 Cup erythritol, half Cup natural peanut butter, quarter tsp sea salt, 1 tsp vanilla extract.

Serves: 8

M.C.: Mixing/Freezing

Procedure: Combine heavy cream, almond milk, cocoa powder, erythritol, sea salt, and vanilla extract in a large bowl. Whisk until well combined and erythritol is dissolved. Pour into an ice cream maker and churn. Midway through churning, add peanut butter to create swirls. Transfer to a freezer container and freeze until set.

N.V.: Offers a balance of creaminess with low carb count, suitable for a ketogenic lifestyle.

7.3 Mango Sorbet (Naturally Sweetened)

Recipe 1: Tropical Mango Lime Sorbet

P.T.: 4 hours 20 mins

Ingr.: 3 Cups ripe mango, cubed and frozen; juice of 2 limes; zest of 1 lime; quarter Cup coconut water; a handful of fresh mint leaves.

Serves: 4

M.C.: Blending/Freezing

Procedure: Blend the frozen mango cubes, lime juice, lime zest, and coconut water until smooth in a food processor. Add mint leaves in the last few pulses to incorporate. Transfer the mixture to a freezer-safe container. Freeze until firm, stirring occasionally. Serve chilled with additional mint for garnish.

N.V.: Rich in vitamins, minerals, and antioxidants.

Recipe 2: Mango Basil Sorbet

P.T.: 4 hours 15 mins

Ingr.: 4 Cups ripe mango, cubed and frozen; quarter Cup fresh basil leaves; juice of 1 lemon; quarter Cup filtered water.

Serves: 6

M.C.: Blending/Freezing

Procedure: In a blender, combine the frozen mango, basil leaves, lemon juice, and filtered water. Blend until the mixture is smooth and creamy. Pour into a freezer-safe container. Freeze, stirring every hour, until the sorbet reaches the desired consistency. Serve garnished with basil leaves.

N.V.: High in vitamin C and A, with no added sugars.

Recipe 3: Spiced Mango Sorbet

P.T.: 5 hours

Ingr.: 3 Cups ripe mango, peeled and frozen; 1 tsp ground ginger; half tsp ground cinnamon; juice of 1 orange; quarter Cup almond milk.

Serves: 4

M.C.: Blending/Freezing

Procedure: Puree the mango, ground ginger, cinnamon, orange juice, and almond milk in a food processor until silky smooth. Transfer to a freezer-safe bowl. Freeze, stirring occasionally to break up ice crystals, until it reaches a scoopable consistency. Serve immediately or store in the freezer.

N.V.: Low in calories, naturally sweetened, with a hint of spice.

Recipe 4: Mango Coconut Sorbet

P.T.: 6 hours

Ingr.: 4 Cups ripe mango, cubed and frozen; half Cup coconut milk (full-fat for creaminess); juice of 2 limes; quarter Cup shredded unsweetened coconut for garnish.

Serves: 5

M.C.: Blending/Freezing

Procedure: Blend the frozen mango, coconut milk, and lime juice until completely smooth. Pour the mixture into a freezer-safe container. Freeze for at least 6 hours or until solid, stirring occasionally if possible. Before serving, let it sit at room temperature for a few mins for easier scooping. Garnish with shredded coconut.

N.V.: Features healthy fats from coconut milk and natural sweetness from mango.

DOWNLOAD YOUR BONUS
Gourmet Breakfast Bliss Guide

Dear Reader,

I want to extend my heartfelt thanks for purchasing this book and downloading the bonus material.

Your support means the world to me.

If you have a moment, I'd greatly appreciate hearing your thoughts.

Your review on Amazon would not only help me improve but also guide others in their reading journey.

Thank you once again for your support!

Warm regards,

Haley Andre

Chapter 8: Puddings and Parfaits

8.1 Chia Seed Pudding (Variety of Flavors)

Recipe 1: Vanilla Bean Chia Pudding

P.T.: 4 hours 10 mins

Ingr.: quarter Cup chia seeds, 1 Cup unsweetened almond milk, half tsp vanilla bean paste, 2 tbsp erythritol (powdered), quarter Cup heavy cream (for topping, optional).

Serves: 2

M.C.: Mixing/Refrigerating

Procedure: In a bowl, whisk together chia seeds, almond milk, vanilla bean paste, and erythritol until well combined. Let sit for 5 mins, then whisk again to prevent clumping. Cover and refrigerate for at least 4 hours, or overnight, until it thickens to a pudding-like consistency. Serve with a dollop of heavy cream, if desired.

N.V.: Rich in omega-3 fatty acids, low in net carbs.

Recipe 2: Berry Bliss Chia Pudding

P.T.: 4 hours 15 mins

Ingr.: quarter Cup chia seeds, 1 Cup coconut milk (full-fat, canned), quarter Cup mixed berries (fresh or frozen, mashed), 2 tbsp monk fruit sweetener, quarter tsp lemon zest (for garnish).

Serves: 2

M.C.: Mixing/Refrigerating

Procedure: Combine chia seeds and coconut milk in a bowl. Stir in mashed berries and monk fruit sweetener until evenly mixed. Let the mixture sit for 5 mins, stir again, then cover and refrigerate until it achieves a pudding consistency, about 4 hours or overnight. Garnish with lemon zest before serving.

N.V.: High in antioxidants, virtually no added sugars.

Recipe 3: Cinnamon Spice Chia Pudding

P.T.: 4 hours 20 mins

Ingr.: quarter Cup chia seeds, 1 Cup almond milk, 1 tsp cinnamon, quarter tsp nutmeg, 2 tbsp erythritol, a pinch of ground cloves, quarter Cup diced apple (for topping).

Serves: 2

M.C.: Mixing/Refrigerating

Procedure: In a mixing bowl, whisk together chia seeds, almond milk, cinnamon, nutmeg, erythritol, and cloves. Allow the mixture to sit for a few mins, then stir again to prevent clumping. Refrigerate for 4 hours or overnight until thickened. Top with diced apple before serving.

N.V.: Low in net carbs, rich in fiber and warming spices.

Recipe 4: Tropical Mango Coconut Chia Pudding

P.T.: 4 hours 25 mins

Ingr.: quarter Cup chia seeds, 1 Cup coconut milk, half Cup mango puree (fresh mango blended until smooth), 2 tbsp erythritol, quarter Cup shredded unsweetened coconut (for topping), a few mint leaves (for garnish).

Serves: 2

M.C.: Mixing/Refrigerating

Procedure: Whisk together chia seeds and coconut milk in a bowl. Stir in mango puree and erythritol until fully incorporated. Let sit for a few mins, then mix again. Cover and refrigerate to set, about 4 hours or overnight. Top with shredded coconut and mint leaves before serving.

N.V.: Features a good source of Vitamin C, low in net carbs.

8.2 Layered Fruit and Yogurt Parfait (Sugar-Free)

Recipe 1: Berry Almond Yogurt Parfait

P.T.: 15 mins

Ingr.: 2 Cups plain Greek yogurt (full-fat), 1 Cup mixed berries (strawberries, blueberries, raspberries), quarter Cup slivered almonds, 2 tbsp chia seeds, 1 tsp vanilla extract, 2 tbsp erythritol (optional, for sweetness).

Serves: 4

M.C.: Layering

Procedure: In a bowl, mix Greek yogurt with vanilla extract and erythritol (if using). In serving glasses, layer yogurt mixture, berries, chia seeds, and almonds. Repeat layers until ingredients are used up. Serve immediately or chill before serving.

N.V.: High in protein, low in net carbs.

Recipe 2: Tropical Coconut Mango Parfait

P.T.: 20 mins

Ingr.: 2 Cups coconut yogurt, 1 Cup diced mango, half Cup unsweetened coconut flakes, quarter Cup macadamia nuts (chopped), 2 tbsp flaxseed meal, 1 tsp lime zest for garnish.

Serves: 4

M.C.: Assembly

Procedure: Start with a layer of coconut yogurt in each serving glass. Add a layer of diced mango, followed by coconut flakes, macadamia nuts, and a sprinkle of flaxseed meal. Repeat the layers. Garnish with lime zest. Serve chilled.

N.V.: Rich in healthy fats, virtually sugar-free.

Recipe 3: Cinnamon Apple Crunch Parfait

P.T.: 10 mins

Ingr.: 2 Cups almond milk yogurt, 1 large apple (diced), half Cup walnuts (chopped), 2 tsp cinnamon, quarter Cup hemp seeds, 2 tbsp powdered erythritol (optional).

Serves: 4

M.C.: Assembling

Procedure: Mix almond milk yogurt with cinnamon and erythritol (if using). Layer yogurt, diced apples, walnuts, and hemp seeds in serving glasses. Repeat the layering process. Finish with a sprinkle of cinnamon on top. Serve immediately or refrigerate.

N.V.: Low in net carbs, high in omega-3s.

Recipe 4: Peach Pecan Yogurt Parfait

P.T.: 15 mins

Ingr.: 2 Cups plain Greek yogurt, 1 Cup fresh peaches (sliced), half Cup pecans (toasted and chopped), 2 tbsp golden flaxseed (ground), 1 tsp almond extract, 2 tbsp monk fruit sweetener (optional).

Serves: 4

M.C.: Layering

Procedure: Stir almond extract and monk fruit sweetener into the Greek yogurt if desired. Begin with a layer of yogurt in each glass, followed by peach slices, a sprinkle of pecans, and golden flaxseed. Repeat layers. Optionally, chill for an hour before serving.

N.V.: Offers a good balance of protein and healthy fats, with minimal impact on blood sugar levels.

8.3 Rich Chocolate Pudding (Avocado-Based)

Recipe 1: Classic Avocado Chocolate Pudding

P.T.: 15 mins

Ingr.: 2 ripe avocados, peeled and pitted; half Cup unsweetened cocoa powder; 1/3 Cup erythritol; half Cup unsweetened almond milk; 1 tsp vanilla extract; a pinch of salt.

Serves: 4

M.C.: Blending

Procedure: Blend avocados, cocoa powder, erythritol, almond milk, vanilla extract, and salt in a food processor until smooth. Adjust sweetness or consistency with a bit more erythritol or almond milk if necessary. Chill for at least 1 hour before serving.

N.V.: High in healthy fats, low in net carbs.

Recipe 2: Mocha Avocado Chocolate Pudding

P.T.: 20 mins

Ingr.: 2 ripe avocados; half Cup unsweetened cocoa powder; 1/3 Cup powdered erythritol; half Cup coconut cream; 2 tsp instant coffee powder; 1 tsp vanilla extract; a pinch of sea salt.

Serves: 4

M.C.: Mixing

Procedure: In a blender, combine all ingredients until the mixture is smooth and creamy. For a more intense coffee flavor, adjust the amount of instant coffee. Chill the pudding in the refrigerator before serving to enhance the flavors.

N.V.: Contains minimal net carbs, rich in potassium and fiber.

Recipe 3: Raspberry Avocado Chocolate Pudding

P.T.: 15 mins

Ingr.: 2 large ripe avocados; half Cup unsweetened cocoa powder; quarter Cup erythritol; half Cup unsweetened almond milk; 1 tsp vanilla extract; half Cup fresh raspberries; a pinch of salt.

Serves: 4

M.C.: Pureeing

Procedure: Puree avocados, cocoa powder, erythritol, almond milk, vanilla extract, and salt until smooth. Gently fold in fresh raspberries or blend them in for a raspberry-flavored pudding. Chill thoroughly before serving.

N.V.: Low in net carbs, high in antioxidants from the raspberries.

Recipe 4: Nutty Avocado Chocolate Pudding

P.T.: 15 mins

Ingr.: 2 ripe avocados; half Cup unsweetened cocoa powder; 1/3 Cup erythritol; half Cup unsweetened almond milk; 1 tsp almond extract; quarter Cup chopped almonds; a pinch of salt.

Serves: 4

M.C.: Blending

Procedure: Combine avocados, cocoa powder, erythritol, almond milk, almond extract, and salt in a blender until creamy. Stir in chopped almonds after blending for a crunchy texture. Refrigerate until chilled and serve garnished with additional chopped almonds.

N.V.: Enhanced with healthy fats and fiber, very low in net carbs.

Chapter 9: Festive Desserts

9.1 Diabetic-Friendly Christmas Yule Log

Recipe 1: Classic Keto Yule Log

P.T.: 1 hour 30 mins

Ingr.: For the cake - 6 eggs (separated), quarter Cup powdered erythritol, half Cup almond flour, quarter Cup cocoa powder, 1 tsp vanilla extract, quarter tsp cream of tartar. For the filling - 1 Cup heavy cream, quarter Cup powdered erythritol, 1 tsp vanilla extract. For the frosting - half Cup unsalted butter, quarter Cup powdered erythritol, 1/3 Cup cocoa powder, 1 tsp vanilla extract.

Serves: 8

M.C.: Baking, Whipping, Frosting

Procedure: Beat egg yolks with erythritol until light. Mix in almond flour and cocoa. In another bowl, beat egg whites and cream of tartar to stiff peaks. Fold into yolk mixture. Spread on a lined baking sheet, bake at 350°F (177°C) for 15 mins. Roll, cool. Whip cream, erythritol, and vanilla for filling. Unroll cake, spread filling, re-roll. For frosting, beat butter, erythritol, cocoa, and vanilla, cover the log. Chill before serving.

N.V.: High in healthy fats, low in net carbs.

Recipe 2: No-Bake Chocolate Peppermint Yule Log

P.T.: 2 hours

Ingr.: For the base - 2 Cups almond flour, 1 Cup unsweetened shredded coconut, half Cup powdered erythritol, half Cup cocoa powder, half Cup melted coconut oil, 1 tsp peppermint extract. For the filling - 1 Cup mascarpone cheese, quarter Cup powdered erythritol, 1 tsp vanilla extract.

Serves: 10

M.C.: Mixing, Freezing

Procedure: Mix almond flour, coconut, erythritol, cocoa, coconut oil, and peppermint. Press into a log shape, freeze 1 hour. Mix mascarpone, erythritol, and vanilla for filling. Slice log lengthwise, spread filling, reassemble. Freeze until set.

N.V.: Low in net carbs, sugar-free.

Recipe 3: Espresso Almond Yule Log

P.T.: 1 hour

Ingr.: For the sponge - 5 eggs (separated), 1/3 Cup powdered erythritol, half Cup almond flour, 2 tbsp instant espresso powder, 1 tsp vanilla extract. For the filling - 1 Cup heavy whipping cream, 2 tbsp powdered erythritol, 1 tsp vanilla extract. For the frosting - half Cup butter, 2 tbsp erythritol, 2 tbsp cocoa powder, 1 tsp espresso powder.

Serves: 8

M.C.: Baking, Whipping, Frosting

Procedure: Beat yolks with erythritol, add almond flour, espresso, vanilla. Beat whites to peaks, fold into yolk mix. Bake as thin layer at 350°F (177°C) for 18 mins. Cool, spread whipped cream, roll. For frosting, mix butter, erythritol, cocoa, espresso. Apply to log. Chill.

N.V.: Rich in flavor, minimal net carbs.

Recipe 4: Nutty Pumpkin Spice Yule Log

P.T.: 1 hour 45 mins

Ingr.: For the cake - 6 eggs (separated), 1/3 Cup powdered erythritol, half Cup pumpkin puree, half Cup almond flour, 1 tsp pumpkin pie spice. For the filling - 1 Cup heavy cream, quarter Cup powdered erythritol, 1 tsp cinnamon. For the frosting - half Cup cream cheese, quarter Cup butter, quarter Cup powdered erythritol, 1 tsp vanilla extract, quarter Cup chopped pecans (for decoration).

Serves: 8

M.C.: Baking, Whipping, Frosting

Procedure: Whip yolks with erythritol, mix in pumpkin, almond flour, spice. Beat whites to peaks, fold in. Bake at 350°F (177°C) for 20 mins. Cool, fill with whipped cream mixed with erythritol and cinnamon, roll. Frost with cream cheese mix, sprinkle pecans. Chill.

N.V.: Keto-friendly, rich in autumn flavors.

9.2 No-Bake Cheesecake (For Easter Celebrations)

Recipe 1: Lemon Berry Keto Cheesecake

P.T.: 4 hours

Ingr.: For the crust - 1.5 Cups almond flour, 1/3 Cup melted coconut oil, 1 tbsp erythritol. For the filling - 2 Cups cream cheese (softened), 1 Cup sour cream, quarter Cup erythritol, zest of 1 lemon, 1 tsp vanilla extract. For the topping - 1 Cup mixed berries (strawberries, blueberries, raspberries).

Serves: 8

M.C.: Mixing/Refrigerating

Procedure: Mix almond flour, coconut oil, and erythritol for the crust, press into a pie dish. Blend cream cheese, sour cream, erythritol, lemon zest, and vanilla until smooth for the filling. Pour over crust, chill for 3 hours. Top with fresh berries before serving.

N.V.: High in healthy fats, minimal net carbs.

Recipe 2: Vanilla Bean Coconut Cheesecake

P.T.: 5 hours

Ingr.: For the crust - 2 Cups shredded unsweetened coconut, quarter Cup coconut oil. For the filling - 2.5 Cups cashews (soaked overnight), half Cup coconut cream, seeds from 1 vanilla bean, quarter Cup powdered erythritol, quarter Cup lemon juice.

Serves: 10

M.C.: Blending/Freezing

Procedure: Process shredded coconut and coconut oil, press into a springform pan. Blend cashews, coconut cream, vanilla bean seeds, erythritol, and lemon juice until creamy. Pour over crust, freeze until set. Let thaw slightly before serving.

N.V.: Rich in fiber and nutrients, very low in carbs.

Recipe 3: Chocolate Hazelnut Cheesecake

P.T.: 6 hours

Ingr.: For the crust - 1.5 Cups ground hazelnuts, quarter Cup cocoa powder, 1/3 Cup melted butter. For the filling - 2 Cups cream cheese, 1 Cup heavy cream, 1/3 Cup powdered erythritol, half Cup unsweetened cocoa powder, 1 tsp vanilla extract.

Serves: 12

M.C.: Mixing/Chilling

Procedure: Mix ground hazelnuts, cocoa, and butter for crust, press into pan. Whip cream cheese, heavy cream, erythritol, cocoa, and vanilla until fluffy for filling. Spread over crust, chill until firm. Optional: garnish with hazelnuts.

N.V.: High in antioxidants, low in net carbs.

Recipe 4: Strawberry Pistachio Cheesecake

P.T.: 4 hours 30 mins

Ingr.: For the crust - 1 Cup pistachios, quarter Cup almond flour, quarter Cup melted coconut oil. For the filling - 2 Cups cream cheese, half Cup powdered erythritol, 1 tsp vanilla extract, 1 Cup diced strawberries. For the garnish - Whole strawberries, chopped pistachios.

Serves: 8

M.C.: Processing/Refrigerating

Procedure: Process pistachios, almond flour, and coconut oil for crust, press into pan. Blend cream cheese, erythritol, and vanilla for filling, fold in diced strawberries. Pour over crust, refrigerate until set. Garnish with strawberries and pistachios.

N.V.: Offers a balance of sweet and nutty flavors, minimal net carbs.

9.3 Pumpkin Spice Custards (Thanksgiving Treat)

Recipe 1: Classic Keto Pumpkin Custard

P.T.: 1 hour

Ingr.: 1.5 Cups pumpkin puree, 1 Cup heavy cream, 3 large eggs, half Cup erythritol, 1 tsp vanilla extract, 2 tsp pumpkin pie spice, a pinch of salt.

Serves: 6

M.C.: Baking

Procedure: Whisk together pumpkin puree, heavy cream, eggs, erythritol, vanilla extract, pumpkin pie spice, and salt until smooth. Pour into ramekins placed in a baking dish. Pour hot water into the baking dish until halfway up the sides of the ramekins. Bake at 350°F (175°C) for 45 mins or until custards are set. Cool before serving.

N.V.: Rich in nutrients, low in net carbs.

Recipe 2: Spiced Coconut Milk Pumpkin Custard

P.T.: 50 mins

Ingr.: 1.5 Cups pumpkin puree, 1 can (13.5 oz) full-fat coconut milk, 4 eggs, half Cup powdered erythritol, 1 tsp cinnamon, half tsp ginger, quarter tsp nutmeg, quarter tsp cloves, a pinch of salt.

Serves: 6

M.C.: Baking

Procedure: Blend all ingredients until smooth. Divide the mixture among ramekins. Place ramekins in a large baking pan, fill the pan with boiling water halfway up the sides of the ramekins. Bake at 325°F (163°C) for 40 mins. Chill before serving.

N.V.: Dairy-free, low in carbs, suitable for a keto diet.

Recipe 3: Nutmeg-Infused Pumpkin Custard

P.T.: 55 mins

Ingr.: 2 Cups pumpkin puree, 3/4 Cup almond milk, 4 eggs, 1/3 Cup erythritol, 2 tsp pumpkin pie spice, 1 tsp vanilla extract, half tsp grated nutmeg, a pinch of salt.

Serves: 6

M.C.: Baking

Procedure: Whisk pumpkin puree, almond milk, eggs, erythritol, pumpkin pie spice, vanilla extract, nutmeg, and salt until thoroughly combined. Pour into greased ramekins. Bake in a water bath at 350°F (177°C) for 50 mins. Serve chilled, garnished with a sprinkle of nutmeg.

N.V.: Low-carb, enhanced with aromatic spices.

Recipe 4: Pumpkin Almond Custard

P.T.: 1 hour 10 mins

Ingr.: 1.5 Cups pumpkin puree, 1 Cup heavy cream, half Cup unsweetened almond milk, 4 eggs, half Cup erythritol, 1 tsp vanilla extract, 2 tsp pumpkin pie spice, a pinch of salt, whipped cream (optional for serving).

Serves: 6

M.C.: Baking

Procedure: Mix pumpkin puree, heavy cream, almond milk, eggs, erythritol, vanilla, pumpkin pie spice, and salt until smooth. Pour the mixture into ramekins. Place ramekins in a baking tray, fill the tray with hot water halfway up the ramekins. Bake at 325°F (163°C) until custards set, about 60 mins. Cool and optionally serve with whipped cream.

N.V.: A perfect blend of creaminess and fall flavors, keto-friendly.

Chapter 10: International Desserts

10.1 Italian Tiramisu (Adjusted for Diabetics)

Recipe 1: Classic Diabetic-Friendly Tiramisu

P.T.: 2 hours 30 mins

Ingr.: 2 Cups strong brewed coffee (cooled), quarter Cup erythritol, 3 large eggs (separated), 1 Cup mascarpone cheese, 1 tsp vanilla extract, 2 tbsp unsweetened cocoa powder, sugar-free ladyfingers (homemade or store-bought).

Serves: 8

M.C.: Assembly

Procedure: Mix coffee with 1 tbsp erythritol. Dip ladyfingers briefly in the coffee mixture and lay them in a dish. Whip egg yolks with 2 tbsp erythritol until creamy, then fold in mascarpone and vanilla. In another bowl, beat egg whites to stiff peaks, then gently fold into the mascarpone mixture. Spread half over the ladyfingers, add another layer of dipped ladyfingers, then finish with the remaining mascarpone. Chill for 2 hours. Dust with cocoa before serving.

N.V.: Low in carbs, suitable for diabetics.

Recipe 2: No-Coffee Berry Tiramisu

P.T.: 2 hours

Ingr.: 2 Cups mixed berries (raspberries and blueberries), quarter Cup erythritol, 1 Cup mascarpone cheese, 3 eggs (separated), 1 tsp vanilla extract, 2 tbsp unsweetened cocoa powder, sugar-free ladyfingers.

Serves: 8

M.C.: Assembly

Procedure: Puree half the berries with 1 tbsp erythritol. Dip ladyfingers in the berry puree and lay them in a dish. Whip egg yolks with erythritol, fold in mascarpone and vanilla. Beat egg whites to stiff peaks, fold into mascarpone. Layer over ladyfingers, add fresh berries, another layer of dipped ladyfingers, and mascarpone. Chill and dust with cocoa.

N.V.: Rich in antioxidants, low in carbs.

Recipe 3: Espresso Walnut Tiramisu

P.T.: 3 hours

Ingr.: 2 Cups decaf espresso (cooled), quarter Cup erythritol, 1 Cup mascarpone, 3 eggs (separated), 1 tsp vanilla extract, half Cup chopped walnuts, sugar-free ladyfingers, 2 tbsp unsweetened cocoa powder.

Serves: 8

M.C.: Assembly

Procedure: Mix espresso with erythritol. Dip ladyfingers in espresso, layer in a dish. Mix egg yolks with erythritol, mascarpone, vanilla. Beat whites to peaks, fold into yolk mix. Layer over ladyfingers, sprinkle with walnuts, add another layer of both. Chill, dust with cocoa.

N.V.: Offers healthy fats, low in carbs.

Recipe 4: Chocolate Orange Tiramisu

P.T.: 2 hours 45 mins

Ingr.: 2 Cups strong brewed decaf coffee, quarter Cup erythritol, 1 Cup mascarpone cheese, 3 eggs (separated), 1 tsp vanilla extract, 1 tsp orange zest, sugar-free ladyfingers, 2 tbsp unsweetened cocoa powder.

Serves: 8

M.C.: Assembly

Procedure: Flavor coffee with orange zest and erythritol. Dip ladyfingers briefly, layer in a dish. Whip yolks with erythritol, fold in mascarpone, vanilla. Beat egg whites to stiff peaks, fold into mascarpone. Layer over ladyfingers, add another layer of both. Chill, dust with cocoa.

N.V.: Low in carbs, diabetic-friendly.

10.2 French Clafoutis with Dark Cherries (Sugar substitute)

Recipe 1: Keto Cherry Clafoutis

P.T.: 45 mins

Ingr.: 2 Cups dark cherries (pitted), 4 eggs, 1 Cup almond milk, 3/4 Cup almond flour, half Cup erythritol, 1 tsp vanilla extract, a pinch of salt, butter (for greasing the pan).

Serves: 8

M.C.: Baking

Procedure: Preheat your oven to 350°F (175°C). Grease a pie dish with butter and distribute cherries evenly at the bottom. Blend eggs, almond milk, almond flour, erythritol, vanilla, and salt until smooth. Pour the batter over cherries. Bake for 35-40 mins until set and lightly golden. Let cool before serving.

N.V.: High in protein and fiber, low in net carbs.

Recipe 2: Coconut Flour Cherry Clafoutis

P.T.: 50 mins

Ingr.: 2 Cups pitted dark cherries, half Cup coconut flour, quarter Cup powdered erythritol, 4 eggs, 1 Cup coconut cream, 1 tsp almond extract, pinch of salt, butter (for greasing).

Serves: 8

M.C.: Baking

Procedure: Grease a baking dish with butter. Scatter cherries at the bottom. Whisk together coconut flour, erythritol, eggs, coconut cream, almond extract, and salt until smooth. Pour over cherries. Bake at 350°F (175°C) for 40-45 mins until golden. Cool slightly before serving.

N.V.: Low carb, gluten-free, and dairy-free.

Recipe 3: Lemon Zest Cherry Clafoutis

P.T.: 55 mins

Ingr.: 2 Cups dark cherries, pitted, 4 large eggs, 1 Cup heavy cream, half Cup erythritol, 2/3 Cup almond flour, zest of 1 lemon, 1 tsp vanilla extract, pinch of salt, butter (for the dish).

Serves: 8

M.C.: Baking

Procedure: Place cherries in a buttered baking dish. Mix eggs, cream, erythritol, almond flour, lemon zest, vanilla, and salt until smooth. Pour this mixture over the cherries. Bake in a preheated oven at 350°F (175°C) for about 45 mins. The clafoutis should be golden and set. Serve warm or at room temperature.

N.V.: Rich in healthy fats, minimal impact on blood sugar levels.

Recipe 4: Dark Chocolate Cherry Clafoutis

P.T.: 1 hour

Ingr.: 2 Cups dark cherries, pitted, 4 eggs, half Cup unsweetened almond milk, 1/3 Cup erythritol, quarter Cup cocoa powder, half Cup almond flour, 1 tsp vanilla extract, a pinch of salt, butter (for greasing), sugar-free dark chocolate shavings (for garnish).

Serves: 8

M.C.: Baking

Procedure: Preheat oven to 350°F (175°C). Butter a pie dish and spread cherries on the bottom. Blend eggs, almond milk, erythritol, cocoa powder, almond flour, vanilla, and salt until smooth. Pour over cherries. Bake for about 45-50 mins. Garnish with chocolate shavings before serving.

N.V.: Offers antioxidants from dark chocolate and cherries, low in carbs.

10.3 Indian Carrot Halwa (Made with Artificial Sweetener)

Recipe 1: Classic Keto Carrot Halwa

P.T.: 30 mins

Ingr.: 4 Cups grated carrots, 1 Cup almond milk, half Cup heavy cream, 1/3 Cup erythritol (or another artificial sweetener of choice), quarter Cup ghee, 1 tsp cardamom powder, a handful of chopped almonds and pistachios for garnish.

Serves: 6

M.C.: Sautéing, Simmering

Procedure: Heat ghee in a pan. Add grated carrots, sauté for 5 mins. Mix in almond milk and cream, cook on medium heat until milk is absorbed, stirring occasionally. Add erythritol and cardamom, cook until mixture thickens. Garnish with nuts before serving warm or chilled.

N.V.: Rich in vitamins, low in net carbs, suitable for a keto diet.

Recipe 2: Vegan Coconut Carrot Halwa

P.T.: 35 mins

Ingr.: 4 Cups grated carrots, 1 Cup coconut milk, quarter Cup coconut oil, 1/3 Cup stevia (granulated), 1 tsp cardamom powder, half Cup shredded unsweetened coconut, a handful of cashews for garnish.

Serves: 6

M.C.: Cooking, Stirring

Procedure: In a large pan, heat coconut oil over medium heat. Add carrots, cook until tender. Stir in coconut milk and stevia, simmer until the mixture thickens. Add cardamom and shredded coconut, cook for an additional 5 mins. Garnish with cashews. Serve warm.

N.V.: Dairy-free, low in carbs, enhanced with healthy fats.

Recipe 3: Saffron-Infused Carrot Halwa

P.T.: 40 mins

Ingr.: 4 Cups grated carrots, 1 Cup almond milk, half Cup heavy cream, quarter Cup ghee, 1/3 Cup erythritol, a pinch of saffron (soaked in 2 tbsp warm milk), 1 tsp cardamom powder, silver leaf for decoration (optional).

Serves: 6

M.C.: Simmering, Stirring

Procedure: Heat ghee in a deep pan, add carrots and sauté until slightly softened. Add almond milk, cream, and saffron milk, cook on low heat until completely absorbed. Stir in erythritol and cardamom, cook until the mixture becomes dense. Decorate with silver leaf. Serve warm or chilled.

N.V.: Luxurious taste with minimal carbs, suitable for special occasions.

Recipe 4: Nutty Carrot Halwa

P.T.: 45 mins

Ingr.: 4 Cups grated carrots, 1 Cup almond milk, half Cup heavy cream, quarter Cup ghee, 1/3 Cup allulose (or another keto-friendly sweetener), 1 tsp cardamom powder, quarter Cup each of chopped walnuts and almonds.

Serves: 6

M.C.: Cooking, Stirring

Procedure: Melt ghee in a pan, add grated carrots. Cook until they start to soften. Add almond milk and cream, simmer until the liquid is absorbed. Stir in sweetener and cardamom, cook until the halwa thickens. Mix in half the nuts, cook for another 5 mins. Garnish with the remaining nuts. Serve warm or cold.

N.V.: Perfect balance of sweetness and nutrition, low in net carbs, high in fiber.

Chapter 11: Smoothies and Drinks

11.1 Green Detox Smoothie (With Spinach and Avocado)

Recipe 1: Classic Spinach Avocado Detox Smoothie

P.T.: 10 mins

Ingr.: 2 Cups fresh spinach, 1 ripe avocado (peeled and pitted), half cucumber (sliced), 1 tbsp chia seeds, 1 Cup unsweetened almond milk, juice of 1 lemon, a few mint leaves for freshness.

Serves: 2

M.C.: Blending

Procedure: Combine all ingredients in a high-speed blender. Blend until smooth. If the smoothie is too thick, add a bit more almond milk to reach your desired consistency. Serve immediately to enjoy the full detox benefits.

N.V.: Rich in Omega-3s, vitamins, and minerals. Low in net carbs.

Recipe 2: Ginger-Lime Green Smoothie

P.T.: 8 mins

Ingr.: 2 Cups spinach leaves, 1 small avocado, half inch ginger (peeled), juice of 2 limes, 1 tbsp flaxseed, 1 Cup coconut water, ice cubes (optional).

Serves: 2

M.C.: Blending

Procedure: Blend spinach, avocado, ginger, lime juice, flaxseed, and coconut water until creamy. Add ice cubes for a chilled smoothie. This blend is perfect for a morning detox and digestive aid.

N.V.: High in fiber, promotes healthy digestion.

Recipe 3: Creamy Kale and Avocado Smoothie

P.T.: 10 mins

Ingr.: 1 Cup kale leaves (stems removed), 1 large avocado, 1 tbsp hemp seeds, juice of 1 lemon, 1 Cup unsweetened almond milk, half Cup ice, pinch of sea salt.

Serves: 2

M.C.: Blending

Procedure: Place kale, avocado, hemp seeds, lemon juice, almond milk, ice, and sea salt in a blender. Process until smooth and creamy. This smoothie combines the detoxifying benefits of kale with the healthy fats of avocado.

N.V.: Loaded with antioxidants and healthy fats.

Recipe 4: Avocado Spinach Protein Smoothie

P.T.: 12 mins

Ingr.: 2 Cups baby spinach, 1 medium avocado, half Cup cucumber, 2 tbsps pumpkin seeds, 1 Cup water or almond milk, juice of half lemon, 1 scoop protein powder (unsweetened, plant-based).

Serves: 2

M.C.: Blending

Procedure: Combine spinach, avocado, cucumber, pumpkin seeds, lemon juice, water/almond milk, and protein powder in a blender. Blend until smooth. This smoothie is perfect for post-workout recovery, providing both protein and essential nutrients.

N.V.: Provides a good balance of protein, healthy fats, and essential vitamins.

11.2 Almond Milk Hot Chocolate (Sugar-Free)

Recipe 1: Classic Creamy Almond Milk Hot Chocolate

P.T.: 10 mins

Ingr.: 2 Cups unsweetened almond milk, quarter Cup unsweetened cocoa powder, quarter Cup erythritol (powdered), half tsp vanilla extract, a pinch of sea salt.

Serves: 2

M.C.: Simmering

Procedure: In a saucepan, whisk together almond milk and cocoa powder over medium heat until fully combined. Add erythritol, vanilla extract, and a pinch of sea salt. Continue to whisk until the mixture is hot but not boiling. Serve warm, optionally topped with whipped coconut cream.

N.V.: Low in calories, contains no added sugars.

Recipe 2: Spiced Almond Milk Hot Chocolate

P.T.: 15 mins

Ingr.: 2 Cups unsweetened almond milk, 3 tbsp unsweetened cocoa powder, quarter Cup erythritol, half tsp cinnamon, quarter tsp nutmeg, 1/8 tsp cayenne pepper (optional), half tsp vanilla extract.

Serves: 2

M.C.: Heating

Procedure: Heat almond milk in a pot over medium heat. Mix cocoa powder, erythritol, cinnamon, nutmeg, and cayenne pepper in a small bowl. Gradually whisk the dry ingredients into the almond milk until smooth. Stir in vanilla extract. Heat until warm, stirring frequently. Serve immediately.

N.V.: Rich in antioxidants, sugar-free.

Recipe 3: Minty Almond Milk Hot Cocoa

P.T.: 12 mins

Ingr.: 2 Cups unsweetened almond milk, quarter Cup unsweetened cocoa powder, quarter Cup erythritol, 1 tsp peppermint extract, whipped cream (sugar-free) for topping.

Serves: 2

M.C.: Whisking

Procedure: Warm almond milk in a saucepan over medium heat. Whisk in cocoa powder and erythritol until there are no lumps. Stir in peppermint extract. Continue to heat until the mixture is thoroughly warm. Pour into mugs and top with sugar-free whipped cream if desired.

N.V.: Zero added sugars, low in carbs.

Recipe 4: Lavender Almond Milk Hot Chocolate

P.T.: 15 mins

Ingr.: 2 Cups unsweetened almond milk, quarter Cup cocoa powder, quarter Cup erythritol, 1 tsp dried lavender flowers, half tsp vanilla extract, a pinch of salt.

Serves: 2

M.C.: Infusing

Procedure: Heat almond milk and lavender over medium heat until hot but not boiling. Remove from heat and let steep for 5 mins. Strain out lavender. Return milk to heat, whisk in cocoa powder, erythritol, vanilla extract, and a pinch of salt. Heat through, stirring until smooth. Serve hot.

N.V.: Calorie-conscious, free from added sugars.

11.3 Berry Blast Smoothie (No Added Sugar)

Recipe 1: Ultimate Berry Almond Smoothie

P.T.: 5 mins

Ingr.: 1 Cup mixed berries (strawberries, blueberries, raspberries, blackberries, frozen), 1 Cup unsweetened almond milk, quarter Cup plain Greek yogurt, 2 tbsp chia seeds, 1 tbsp almond butter, 1 tsp vanilla extract.

Serves: 2

M.C.: Blending

Procedure: Combine all ingredients in a blender. Blend on high until smooth and creamy. If the smoothie is too thick, add a bit more almond milk to reach your desired consistency. Serve immediately for a refreshing, nutrient-packed treat.

N.V.: Rich in antioxidants, vitamins, and minerals. High in fiber and protein, low in net carbs.

Recipe 2: Berry Avocado Glow Smoothie

P.T.: 5 mins

Ingr.: 1 Cup mixed berries (frozen), 1 ripe avocado, 1 Cup spinach leaves, 1 Cup coconut water, 1 tbsp flaxseed meal, 1 tsp lemon juice.

Serves: 2

M.C.: Pureeing

Procedure: Add all ingredients to a blender and puree until smooth. The avocado adds creaminess and healthy fats, making this smoothie not only delicious but also incredibly satisfying. Perfect for a morning boost or a midday snack.

N.V.: Loaded with omega-3 fatty acids, virtually sugar-free.

Recipe 3: Refreshing Berry Mint Smoothie

P.T.: 5 mins

Ingr.: 1.5 Cups mixed berries (frozen), 1 Cup unsweetened almond milk, half Cup cucumber (chopped), a handful of fresh mint leaves, 1 tbsp hemp seeds, ice cubes (optional).

Serves: 2

M.C.: Blending

Procedure: Blend berries, almond milk, cucumber, mint leaves, and hemp seeds until smooth. Add ice cubes for an extra chilled smoothie. This blend is particularly refreshing and perfect for cooling down on a hot day or after a workout.

N.V.: High in plant-based protein, low in carbs, and no added sugar.

Recipe 4: Berry Ginger Zing Smoothie

P.T.: 6 mins

Ingr.: 1 Cup frozen mixed berries, 1 Cup unsweetened green tea (cooled), half inch fresh ginger (peeled), 1 tbsp pumpkin seeds, half tsp ground turmeric, 1 tbsp lemon juice.

Serves: 2

M.C.: Blending

Procedure: Combine berries, green tea, ginger, pumpkin seeds, turmeric, and lemon juice in a blender. Blend until smooth. The ginger and turmeric add a zesty kick and anti-inflammatory benefits, while the berries and lemon provide a natural sweetness and a vitamin C boost.

N.V.: Anti-inflammatory properties, no added sugars, and packed with nutrients.

Chapter 12: Conclusion

12.1 Embracing a Sweet Life Without Sugar

Living without sugar does not mean living without sweetness. In this journey, we discover the richness of flavors and the abundance of health benefits that come with choosing alternatives to sugar. This chapter delves into the transformative experience of embracing a life without sugar, highlighting the innovative ways to enjoy sweet treats while maintaining health and wellness.

The Paradigm Shift: Begin with discussing the initial challenge of eliminating sugar from the diet, highlighting the prevalent role sugar plays in modern eating habits. Emphasize the health risks associated with excessive sugar consumption, such as diabetes, obesity, and heart disease, underscoring the importance of this dietary change.

The Discovery of Alternatives: Introduce readers to the world of natural sweeteners like stevia, erythritol, and monk fruit extract. Describe how these alternatives provide the sweetness people crave without the negative health impacts of sugar. Mention the advances in food technology that have made these substitutes more accessible and palatable than ever before.

The Transformation of Taste: Discuss how reducing sugar consumption can reset taste preferences, making foods taste naturally sweeter over time. Share personal anecdotes or testimonials that highlight how flavors become more vibrant and nuanced when not masked by the overpowering sweetness of sugar.

Health Benefits Galore: Outline the numerous health benefits that come with reducing sugar intake. Include improvements in energy levels, weight management, and reduced risk of chronic diseases. Use scientific studies and expert opinions to bolster these claims, providing a compelling argument for the sugar-free lifestyle.

The Joy of Cooking and Baking: Dive into the creative aspect of preparing sugar-free treats. Offer tips for substituting sugar in recipes, such as adjusting liquid ratios or adding spice to enhance flavor. Encourage readers to experiment with sugar-free recipes, emphasizing that this journey can be a culinary adventure full of delicious discoveries.

Community and Support: Highlight the importance of finding support among friends, family, and online communities. Share stories of how shared experiences and tips can make transitioning to a sugar-free lifestyle more manageable and enjoyable.

The Bigger Picture: Connect the personal benefits of a sugar-free lifestyle with broader societal implications, such as the potential for reduced healthcare costs and a healthier population. Discuss how individual choices can lead to collective benefits, inspiring readers to consider the impact of their dietary decisions.

A Life of Balance: Acknowledge that living sugar-free doesn't mean never enjoying a sweet treat again. Discuss the concept of balance and moderation, suggesting ways to incorporate occasional treats into a healthy lifestyle without reverting to old habits.

Embracing the Journey: Conclude by reflecting on the journey of embracing a life without sugar as one of empowerment and self-discovery. Encourage readers to view this change not as a restriction, but as an opportunity to enhance their health, explore new flavors, and live a fuller life.

12.2 The Importance of Portion Control

In a world where excess is often the norm, the concept of portion control emerges as a beacon of balance and moderation, especially in managing a diabetes-friendly diet. Portion control is not merely a strategy; it's a fundamental aspect of a healthy lifestyle that fosters a deeper understanding and connection with the food we consume. It transcends the basic notion of reducing the amount of food on our plates, guiding us towards a more mindful, intentional approach to eating.

Begin by demystifying what portion control truly means. It's not about restrictive diets or depriving oneself but about learning to eat in a way that nourishes the body without overindulgence. Explain the difference between portion size and serving size, emphasizing the significance of recognizing how much food is enough for maintaining a healthy balance.

Delve into how portion control directly impacts blood sugar levels, weight management, and overall diabetic health. Highlight the challenges individuals with diabetes face when it comes to managing their diet and how controlling portions can be a powerful tool in their arsenal. Include insights from nutritional science that support the importance of portion control in preventing blood sugar spikes and managing insulin sensitivity.

Offer readers practical strategies for implementing portion control in their daily lives. This could include tips like using smaller plates, understanding food labels, measuring servings with common objects, and the importance of regular, mindful eating habits. Encourage the practice of listening to one's body and recognizing the signals for hunger and fullness.

Address the psychological barriers to portion control, such as emotional eating, the habit of finishing everything on the plate, and the influence of social and cultural norms on eating behavior. Discuss ways to overcome these challenges, perhaps by fostering a healthier relationship with food, understanding the triggers for overeating, and the role of mindfulness in eating.

Eating out or celebrating at social gatherings can present challenges to portion control. Provide advice on navigating these situations without feeling isolated or deprived. Suggestions might include scanning menus in advance, sharing meals, choosing healthier options, and focusing on the social experience over the food.

Illuminate the long-term benefits of adopting portion control, not just for individuals with diabetes but for anyone seeking a healthier lifestyle. Discuss how portion control contributes to sustained weight loss, improved metabolic health, and a greater enjoyment of food. Stress that portion control is a sustainable practice, not a temporary diet.

Share success stories and testimonials from individuals who have successfully incorporated portion control into their lives. Highlight the positive changes they've experienced, both physically and emotionally. This human element can inspire and motivate readers to embark on their own journey of portion control.

Conclude with a powerful call to action, encouraging readers to embrace portion control as a key component of their diabetes management plan and overall wellness strategy. Emphasize that with the right knowledge, tools, and mindset, anyone can master the art of portion control.

12.3 Incorporating Natural Sweetness

In the culinary journey of managing diabetes, embracing natural sweetness is akin to discovering a hidden treasure within nature's bounty. This chapter delves into the transformative approach of leveraging the innate sweetness found in fruits, vegetables, and other natural sources to enhance the flavor profile of diabetic-friendly desserts without compromising blood sugar levels. Moving beyond artificial sweeteners and processed sugars opens up a realm of possibilities, where the natural sugars present in foods provide not just sweetness but also a host of nutritional benefits.

The exploration begins with understanding the glycemic index (GI) and glycemic load (GL) – critical tools in the diabetic diet that measure how food impacts blood sugar levels. Fruits like berries, cherries, and apples, with their lower GI, emerge as excellent choices for imparting natural sweetness to desserts. Their inclusion not only satisfies the sweet tooth but also enriches the body with essential vitamins, minerals, and fibers, which aid in the overall management of diabetes.

Moreover, the versatility of vegetables in adding subtle sweetness and depth to dishes is uncovered. From the earthy undertones of sweet potatoes and carrots to the mild, almost sugary hints in beets, these vegetables become the backbone of numerous recipes, offering a complexity of flavors that refined sugars could never achieve. The art of caramelizing these vegetables to unlock their natural sugars is highlighted, showcasing how a simple cooking process can transform a humble ingredient into a powerhouse of flavor.

The narrative then transitions to the nutritional powerhouse of nuts and seeds, which, when combined with the natural sweetness of fruits and vegetables, create a symphony of textures and tastes. Almonds, chia seeds, and flaxseeds not only provide a crunchy contrast to the softness of baked goods and smoothies but also contribute healthy fats and proteins, making each bite a balanced morsel of goodness.

In weaving the story of natural sweetness into the fabric of diabetic-friendly cooking, the chapter emphasizes the importance of balance and moderation. It acknowledges that while fruits and certain vegetables offer a healthier alternative to processed sugars, their consumption still requires mindfulness and portion control to maintain optimal blood sugar levels.

The narrative is rich with practical tips and tricks for incorporating natural sweetness into everyday cooking. Suggestions on how to ripen fruits to their peak sweetness, roasting nuts to enhance their flavor, or using spices like cinnamon and vanilla to add warmth and depth to dishes without additional sugar, equip readers with the knowledge to experiment confidently in their kitchens.

Personal anecdotes and testimonials interspersed throughout the chapter bring the discussion to life, offering real-world insights into how individuals have successfully integrated natural sweetness into their diets. These stories serve as a source of inspiration, demonstrating that a diabetes diagnosis does not equate to a life devoid of delicious, sweet treats.

12.4 Looking Ahead

Innovation in diabetic care and nutrition is moving at an unprecedented pace. Each day, researchers, nutritionists, and culinary experts are uncovering new ways to make diabetic-friendly ingredients more accessible, more versatile, and more delicious. The horizon is bright with the promise of novel sweeteners derived from natural sources, offering the sweetness we crave without the glycemic impact. Imagine sweetening your favorite desserts with extracts that mimic the taste of sugar, yet are completely metabolized by the body without affecting blood sugar levels.

The future also promises a revolution in how we understand the individualized nature of diabetes management. With advancements in technology, we are moving towards a more personalized approach to dietary planning. Wearable devices and smart technology will allow us to monitor our glycemic response in real-time, tailoring our diet to our body's specific needs. This precision in managing diabetes will not only enhance our control over the disease but will also liberate us to enjoy a broader range of foods, knowing exactly how they impact our body.

Moreover, the globalization of food culture is bringing a wealth of diabetic-friendly culinary traditions to the forefront. From the Mediterranean's rich use of healthy fats and whole grains to the traditional Indian use of complex spices to enhance natural sweetness, the global culinary landscape is a treasure trove of inspiration. As these culinary traditions become more integrated into mainstream diets, they bring with them a variety of flavors and ingredients that enrich the diabetic diet.

Education and awareness are key to embracing this future. As we look ahead, there is a growing movement towards educating people about the importance of diet in managing diabetes. Schools, communities, and online platforms are increasingly offering resources to help individuals make informed dietary choices. This democratization of knowledge empowers everyone to take control of their health through informed food choices.

"Looking Ahead" is an invitation to imagine a world where managing diabetes does not mean sacrificing the joy of eating. It is a world where innovation, personalization, global culinary traditions, and education converge to offer a vibrant, delicious, and healthful eating experience. It is a future where we are not limited by our condition but are empowered to live our lives to the fullest, one diabetic-friendly dish at a time. As we close this chapter and look to the future, let us carry forward the lessons learned, the optimism for what's to come, and the unwavering belief that managing diabetes can be a delicious journey. The path ahead is bright with possibilities, flavors, and the sweet promise of a healthier, happier life.